KEYNES AND ECONOMIC DEVELOPMENT

KEYNES AND ECONOMIC DEVELOPMENT

*The Seventh Keynes Seminar
held at the
University of Kent at Canterbury, 1985*

Edited by

A. P. THIRLWALL

*Professor of Applied Economics
University of Kent at Canterbury*

St Martin's Press   New York

© The Macmillan Press Ltd., 1987

First published in the United States of America in 1987

Printed in Hong Kong

ISBN 0-312-45199-7

Library of Congress Cataloging-in-Publication Data
Keynes Seminar (7th : 1985 : University of Kent at
Canterbury)
Keynes and economic development.
Includes index.
1. Keynesian economics—Congresses. 2. Developing
countries—Economic conditions—Congresses. 3. Develop-
ing countries—Economic policy—Congresses. 4. Keynes,
John Maynard, 1883–1946—Congresses. I. Thirlwall, A. P.
II. Title.
HB99.7.K388   1987   338.9   86-13843
ISBN 0-312-45199-7

Contents

List of Guests and Speakers

Dr M. Ambrosi	*University of Berlin*
Mr G. Bird	*University of Surrey*
Mr S. Brickell	*Folkestone*
Professor W. Carr	*University of Sheffield*
Mr D. Crabtree	*University of Kent*
Professor W. Elkan	*Brunel University*
Mr T. M. Farmiloe	*London*
Mr S. Frowen	*University of Surrey*
Mr E. R. G. Heath, M.P.	*London*
Professor C. Hession	*Brooklyn College, New York*
Mr T. L. Higgins, M.P.	*London*
Mr J. J. Hughes	*University of Kent*
Dr M. Keynes	*Cambridge*
Mr S. Keynes	*London*
Dr I. Little	*Oxford*
Professor W. Newlyn	*Stratford-on-Avon*
Professor W. B. Reddaway	*University of Cambridge*
Sir Austin Robinson	*University of Cambridge*
Professor G. L. S. Shackle	*Aldeburgh, Suffolk*
Professor R. Skidelsky	*University of Warwick*
Professor H. Singer	*University of Sussex*
Professor A. P. Thirlwall	*University of Kent*
Professor J. Toye	*University of Swansea*
Professor M. Vile	*University of Kent*
Dr J. Williamson	*Washington*

Acknowledgements

The editor wishes to thank the Centre for the Study of Cartoons and Caricature, Canterbury, for permission to use the David Low cartoon on the jacket, the Controller of her Majesty's Stationery Office for permission to reproduce the extract from Cmd. 6437, April 1943, and Mrs Pauline Taylor for transcribing the tapes of the seminar and typing the final draft of the manuscript.

A. P. THIRLWALL

Foreword

It was a source of great pleasure to welcome a large audience to the Seventh Keynes Seminar on 15 November 1985. First established by the College in 1972, the Seminars have proved a felicitous way of commemorating the life of Lord Maynard Keynes, giving a richly diverse audience from the University, the City of Canterbury and farther afield the opportunity to hear leading scholars discuss aspects of his life and work. The Seminar Committee has placed considerable stress on continuity in participants, and it is pleasing to place on record that many of those who gathered in 1985 had been present on many previous occasions. There is indeed a growing sense of the inappropriate ness of the College extending to them an invitation to attend the Seminar, for in a very real way they have become the Seminar. It is, I hope, not invidious to single out in this respect Sir Austin Robinson, who contributed to the first of the Seminars and whose presence is a vivid reminder of the intellectual ferment surrounding Keynes. It is appropriate, too, to express appreciation for the unfailing interest which Dr Milo Keynes and Mr Stephen Keynes take in the Seminars.

In formulating the idea of holding such Seminars the first Master of the College, Professor Robert Spence, expressed the conviction that the many facets of Lord Keynes' thought and writings would afford an ample supply of themes – and this has proved the case. If Keynesianism is no longer the unchallenged orthodoxy of our society, it still stands as a towering body of thought, laying great claim to our intellectual and moral assent. For there can be no doubt about his relevance to the great public and political debate of our day, nor can there be doubt about the moral imperatives and the moral values which lay so central to all his thinking. That the goods valued by men should be more widely distributed and that this should be furthered by intelligent international cooperation was a deeply held conviction: our theme of 'Keynes and Economic Development' is testimony to this.

In conclusion, I would like to express the gratitude of the College to the Vice-Chancellor and the Dean and Faculty of Social Sciences for assistance in mounting the Seminar, and to Mr Tim Farmiloe and Macmillan for their constant encouragement and cooperation. The Seminar Committee is greatly indebted to Professor Thirlwall for editing these Proceedings and for so much of the organisation of the Seminar.

Keynes College

Derek Crabtree
Master

Session I

INTRODUCTION
J. J. Hughes (Chairman)

Today's Seminar takes as its theme 'Keynes and Economic Development'. Although Keynes' seminal work *The General Theory of Employment, Interest and Money* was not concerned with the development problem, many of the concepts and techniques of analysis developed in the *General Theory*, and by a succeeding generation of Keynesian economists, are of considerable relevance to our understanding of economic development. Nevertheless, despite our greater understanding of the process of economic development, the gap between rich and poor countries of the world still remains staggering. In 1981, for example, there were about fifty countries whose national income per capita was less than US$320 per year, compared with the United Kingdom's own $9,100 per capita per year, and a figure of $12,100 for the United States itself. Despite the problems that arise when cross-country comparisons of GNP are made, these figures do suggest that we still live in a world that is divided between the 'haves' and the 'have nots'. And the figures serve to remind those of us who are preoccupied with the performance of the British economy that our own problems are not all that great when seen in a somewhat wider perspective.

The two main speakers for the first session this afternoon have both distinguished themselves in the field of applied economics research; they are both Keynesians, and they have both had considerable experience of developing countries and the problems that they face.

Professor Brian Reddaway, who will speak second, might be regarded as a direct descendant of Alfred Marshall, the founding

1

father of modern economics. Marshall held the Chair of Political Economy at Cambridge at the turn of the century while Reddaway occupied it during the period 1969-80. But, of course, the link between the two is not just that they held the same professorial chair at Cambridge; the link is Keynes himself who was a pupil of Marshall and a teacher of the young Reddaway. In addition to holding the Chair of Political Economy, Reddaway was for many years Director of the Department of Applied Economics at Cambridge, and he has held many other appointments including the editorship of the prestigious *Economic Journal*. His publications are far too numerous for me to recite in full this afternoon, but two of his books are of particular relevance to economic development. These are *The Economics of a Declining Population* which was published in 1939, and *The Development of the Indian Economy* published in 1962.

Our first speaker this afternoon is Professor Tony Thirlwall who is a member of Keynes College. Professor Thirlwall came to the University of Kent in 1966, and although this does not quite make him one of the founding fathers of the University he is, I believe, the longest serving member of the Economics Board and, therefore, he can justly be regarded as the father of Kent economics. He has done much to establish and to enhance the reputation of economics at Kent through a stream of papers and books over the past nineteen years or so, including *Financing Economic Development, Inflation Saving and Growth in Developing Countries*, and *Growth and Development* now in its third edition. The last title sells steadily in the developing countries thereby ensuring not only a modest royalty for its author, but also, and more importantly, that students in these developing countries are brought into contact with Tony Thirlwall's ideas on economic development. He has first-hand experience of several countries, including the Sudan and Malaysia. He is a staunch defender of the Keynesian tradition and is highly critical of those who deviate from its orthodoxy. He is, I believe, the ideal person to get today's proceedings off to a good start, and therefore I have pleasure in introducing Professor Tony Thirlwall to you.

KEYNES, ECONOMIC DEVELOPMENT
AND THE DEVELOPING COUNTRIES
A.P. Thirlwall

INTRODUCTION

By almost any measure one cares to take, there are deep economic and social schisms in the world economy. Moreover, there are powerful 'natural' and institutional mechanisms perpetuating and even widening these divisions. The largest rift is undoubtedly between average living standards in the industrialised countries of the northern hemisphere and those prevailing the majority of countries in the southern hemisphere in Asia, Africa and Latin America – aptly called the North–South divide. According to the latest statistics from the World Bank (*World Development Report*, 1985), the average level of per capita income in the developed industrialised countries is over US$11,000 per annum compared to $260 in 35 very low income countries and $1,300 in 59 middle income countries. There are poor people in the developed countries, but there need not be; this is largely the result of social and political choices. There are rich people in the poor countries, but relatively few, and a radical redistribution of income by itself would make very little direct difference to the economic destiny of the average citizen. There are nearly three billion people in the world today living in primary poverty, and one billion of them suffer various states of malnourishment. As far as one can tell, the situation is deteriorating rather than improving. It is true that in most countries average living standards are rising slowly, but because of population growth the absolute numbers in primary poverty are increasing, and the world distribution of income shows no sign of equalising. If the Gini ratio is taken as the measure of income distribution, the ratio is just over 0.6, no lower than it was forty years ago, and far higher than for most domestic income distributions, which in the industrialised countries gives a ratio of about 0.3. The catching up process is colossal. If the average per capita income of today's developing countries is taken as US$800 per annum, it will take over eighty years growing at 3 per cent per annum to catch up with current living standards in the 'north'. It would take a growth rate of 18 per cent for per capita incomes in the 'north' and 'south' to be equalised by the year 2000.

It is easily forgotten, of course, that the rich–poor country divide is a relatively recent phenomenon. All countries were once at subsistence level, and as recently as 250 years ago, at the advent of the British industrial revolution, absolute differences in living standards cannot have been very great. Keynes himself re-minds us, in an article on population published in 1922 (Keynes, 1922), that, historically speaking, belief in the material progress of mankind is quite new. During the greater part of history such a belief was neither compatible with experience nor encouraged by religion. For centuries there was hardly any progress in the material prosperity of mankind, with the lot of the average labourer oscillating around subsistence level in true Malthusian fashion. The idea that the division of labour, or science, might lead to a progressive, cumulative improvement was quite alien. It was not until the eighteenth century that material progress commenced over wide areas in selected parts of Europe – a phenomenon still not fully understood by economic historians but clearly associated with the process of industrialisation – and it was not until 1850 or thereabouts that progress became rapid. The concentrated impact of industrialisation on living standards in the 'north' can be illustrated dramatically with the analogy that if 6000 years of man's 'civilised' existence prior to 1850 is viewed as a day, the last century or so represents less than half an hour, yet in this time more real output had been produced in the developed countries than in the whole of the preceding era (Patel, 1964).

Keynes once assigned to economists the role of the trustees of the *possibility* of civilisation (Harrod, 1951, p. 194). One may be forgiven for wondering whether the current generation of economists have not abrogated this role. We seem to live in an age of unprecedented economic barbarism (or should I say philistinism?) both from the point of view of conduct of domestic economic policy (at least in many countries) and from the point of view of the conduct of international economic relations; a philistinism and chaos that would have appalled Keynes. Some years ago, Arnold Toynbee remarked that

> our age will be remembered not for its horrifying crimes nor its astonishing inventions, but because it is the first generation since the dawn of history in which mankind dared to believe it practical to make the benefits of civilisation available to the whole human race.

Keynes played a major role in this process and in generating the spirit of optimism that pervaded the international economic scene in the immediate post-war years. World economic conditions, of course, have changed, but I now sense a profound spirit of pessimism and lack of self-confidence among economists and policy makers in the ability to design cooperative policies and institutions which will spread the world's income more equitably across the human race. This is very much to be regretted. Third world poverty and economic development not only presents a moral challenge but also in many ways an intellectual challenge equivalent to the challenge of mass unemployment and poverty in the midst of plenty in the 1920s and 1930s which attracted so many brilliant minds to the social sciences, including many of Keynes' disciples. The nature of the challenge, however, is rather different. In the inter-war years, Keynes' task was to provide a theory to fit the facts; to cast aside a model of the workings of the economy that denied the existence of mass unemployment. This he did, and according to the theory the solution to mass unemployment turned out to be costless; expand demand by creating credit and bring idle resources into play. As far as economic development is concerned, however, there is no theoretical lacuna. There is no divorce of the main theories of long-run growth and development from the facts; poor countries need to augment both the quantity and quality of the factors of production. The debates in development economics relate to which factors are most crucial, how to provide them, and to the best form of economic organisation which will maximise the efficiency with which resources are used. Development economics is a relatively new branch of economics. Hirschman (1981) traces the birth to around the time of the Second World War, stemming from a rejection of monoeconomics on the one hand (i.e. the idea that a single economics is applicable to all states of nature) and of neo-Marxism on the other which asserted that economic relations between rich and poor countries could only lead to the perpetuation of underdevelopment. On this hypothesis Keynes might be considered one of the founders of development economics in that having broken the monoeconomics of classical theory in the macro field, it was a natural step to argue that conventional economic theory (in this case neo-classical economics) is inapplicable to poor backward agrarian societies. Hans Singer (1982) has said in a delightful paper of reminiscences that

> as a student of Keynes during the formative years of the General Theory (1934-36) at Cambridge, I was certainly intellectually preconditioned to think in terms of different rules of the game applying to developing countries and the idea of non-orthodox policies in relation to them.

Singer also believes that Keynes' interest in state intervention preconditioned him to take a direct interest in the problems of development planning which became very fashionable after the Second World War, and which was adopted very seriously by the Eastern European countries and by India.

Keynes never wrote a treatise on economic development. It has been suggested (Johnson, 1978) that Keynes' only major work in what now would be called development economics was his book *Indian Currency and Finance* (1913) stemming from his time at the India Office 1906–8. I will not dwell on India here (see Appendix) except to say that Keynes's period at the India Office was but a brief interlude in his life which had nothing to do with a particular interest in India or in poor colonies in general. Keynes appeared to view colonialism as entirely beneficial and he seemed also to deprecate India's desire for industrialisation. He went to the India Office in 1906 having come second to Otto Niemeyer in the Civil Service examinations, and the India Office was regarded as the second best Home Department to the Treasury which Niemeyer chose. Keynes was thoroughly bored there. He wrote to an Eton friend, Page that 'all he had succeeded in doing in two years was shipping one pedigree bull to Bombay' (Harrod, 1951).[1] *Indian Currency and Finance* was published some time after his resignation from the Civil Service in 1908, just before the Indian Finance and Currency Commission was set up in 1913 on which Keynes was first invited to be Secretary and then a full member. The book was not really about economic development; it was more than anything a technical treatise on the intricacies of the Indian monetary system – a system of byzantine complexity which required the genius of Keynes to unravel and elucidate. At that time he was very impressed with the gold exchange standard, and it is sometimes argued that it was Keynes's conversion to the gold exchange standard in those days that led him to support this as the basis of the Bretton Woods system in 1944, over thirty years later. The text supporting this view comes from a paper on the Indian Currency Question that Keynes read to the Royal Economic Society in May 1911 which was never published. It says:

I will endeavour to give reasons for thinking that the existing system to which the name Gold Exchange Standard has been given is something much more civilised, much more economical and much more satisfactory than a gold currency. I should like to see it established in India on a permanent basis and all talk of an eventual gold currency definitely abandoned. The government of India has been the first to adopt the Gold Exchange Standard on a large scale. But every year there are fresh converts; nor will it be long before it becomes, in effect, the standard of half the world. And out of it, in my belief, will be evolved the ideal currency of the future. (Johnson, 1971, p. 69)

John Williamson (1983) is not convinced that the gold exchange standard evolved at Bretton Woods can be traced to *Indian Currency and Finance*, but it is worth remembering Keynes's own quip that 'practical men, who believe themselves to be quite exempt from any intellectual influences, are usually the slaves of some defunct economist' (Keynes, 1936) – in this case, himself! Whatever its origins, it was the gold exchange standard that served the world so well for a quarter of a century, although as Robert Triffin warned prophetically in 1960 (Triffin, 1960) it contained unfortunately the seeds of its own destruction.

Although Keynes may not have written a treatise on economic development, he addressed himself to several development issues and clearly had a vision of the long-run development process and the conduct of international economic relations for maximisation of the global welfare. He has also exerted an indirect influence on development thinking through the application of his ideas by various of his disciples: Joan Robinson and disguised unemployment; Harrod and dynamic economics, and the post-Keynesian emphasis on capital accumulation and planned industrialisation (Johnson, 1978). Before taking up some of these themes, however, let us briefly consider what we mean by economic development and consider some of the forces that perpetuate the development gap.

Per capita income is used as a convenient index of the level of economic development, but the process of development embraces much more than a sustained increase in the average level of per capita income. What is happening to the internal distribution of income and to the performance of other economic and social indicators such as literacy and life expectancy, is also important, as well as what is happening to the state of more intangible values such as justice and freedom. There can be no single all embracive definition of development that would satisfy all people, but I have always been attracted by Goulet's choice of three basic components or core values which any definition of development must embrace: what he calls life sustenance; self-esteem, and freedom (Goulet, 1971). Life sustenance is axiomatic; self-esteem is concerned with the feeling of self-respect and independence, and freedom has to do with choice. No man is free who cannot choose. Goulet's approach embraces the basic needs approach to development pioneered and implemented by the World Bank (with which I broadly sympathise as far as its lending policies are concerned) and also Amartya Sen's new vision of development defined in terms of the expansion of people's entitlements and capabilities, the former giving life sustenance and self-esteem; the latter giving freedom (Sen, 1984). The focus and stress on expanding entitlements and capabilities for all the people (as the closest approximation to the concept of the standard of living) is a natural extension of the earlier switch in development thinking away from growth maximisation *per se* to concern with the structure of production and consumption and the distribution of income. Sen's dissent is that income is often a very inadequate measure of entitlement which depends not only on the ability to sell labour and on the price of commodities in the market but also on such factors as power relations in society; the spatial distribution of resources, and what individuals can extract from the state. In this respect, Sen contends that malnutrition and famine depend as much on entitlements as on lack of income (Sen, 1981).

The depressive and cumulative forces operating to keep people in primary poverty and to perpetuate the development gap between rich and poor countries are several. First we must understand the fundamental theoretical difference between land-based economic activities on the one hand and industrial activities on the other. Land-based activities, in which developing countries tend to specialise, are subject to diminishing returns and produce goods with a low income elasticity of demand, while industrial activities, in which developed countries tend to specialise, are subject to increasing returns and produce goods with a higher income elasticity of demand. The implications of these differences are profound and can in large part account for the differences in living standards that have arisen between 'north' and 'south'. Diminishing returns depresses the level and growth of productivity and means that there is a limit to the profitable employment of labour in these activities, while increasing returns raises the level and growth of productivity and by increasing per capita income enlarges the demand for other commodities in a cumulative expansionary process. In a trading environment, a low income elasticity of demand for land-based products compared to industrial products means that the balance of trade for the regions that produce land-based goods is always likely to deteriorate relative to the regions trading industrial products. These characteristics and mechanisms are the core features of so-called centre–periphery models of growth and development. The 'north–south' divide is living proof, and serves as a permanent reminder, that we do not live in an equilibrium world in which social and economic forces in situations of disequilibrium work towards equilibrium, as Gunnar Myrdal forcefully reminded us many years ago (Myrdal, 1957).

Population growth in the Third World may also be a depressive force. 'The rich countries get richer and the poor countries get children' is a familiar cliché, but I do not place so much emphasis on this factor as others might do. The historical and statistical evidence is equivocal over whether rapid population growth is an impediment or a stimulus to economic progress. In a purely arithmetic sense, of course, and other things remaining the same, rapid population growth must depress the rate of growth of income *per head* by more than slow population growth, but rapid population growth may also stimulate income growth by a variety of mechanisms which leaves the effect on per capita income growth neutral. A lot depends on the environment in which rapid population growth takes place. While Asia may be over-populated; Africa might be said to be under-populated, notwithstanding the current famine. But population growth not only affects per capita income growth, it also affects other dimensions of human welfare such as congestion and overcrowding;

unemployment, and the distribution of income. Given the uncertainty of the population growth–living standard relationship, it is probably wiser to run the risk of type II error and proceed with population control programmes on the assumption that they will improve living standards, rather than to do nothing and contribute to further unemployment; the overcrowding of cities and so on. Keynes himself took an interest in the relation between population and economic welfare, and I shall say more on this subject later when I discuss Keynes's writings on economic development.

The nature of technology and technology transfer is another element in the economic schism. The low level of technology in developing countries, particularly in agriculture, is a major source of low productivity, while the nature of technological transfer from developed to developing countries in industry, which has led to inappropriate techniques of production and products, is a major source of urban unemployment and a distorted pattern of economic development. It used to be thought that capital intensive techniques had lower capital: output ratios and higher profit ratios than labour intensive techniques, but research has shown (Pack, 1982) that extensive substitution possibilities exist which would not impair the level of output or saving providing cooperating factors exist to work with extra labour. A precondition for the use of more appropriate labour intensive techniques, however, is the development of indigenous capital goods industries within the developing countries themselves where the relevant techniques can be designed (Stewart, 1972). The foreign ownership of many industries in developing countries may also not be in the countries' long-run interests, but I will leave this sensitive minefield alone.[2]

A futher depressive tendency which afflicts poor countries is the long-run deterioration in the prices of the primary commodities which they export relative to the prices of industrial goods which they import, which reduces real income directly. This terms of trade effect is sometimes called the Prebisch-Singer thesis after both Raul Prebisch and Hans Singer pointed in separate analyses at the same time in 1950 to this pernicious secular tendency (Prebisch, 1950; Singer, 1950). Prebisch's research on historical import and export prices for the United Kingdom (as the major importer of primary products and exporter of manufactures) put the percentage deterioration at 0.9 per cent per annum. The historical secular decline is confirmed by Spraos (1980), and from my own research (Thirlwall and Bergevin, 1985) I can confirm that, excluding petroleum, the secular decline has continued in the years since 1954. For primary products exported by less developed countries, the percentage decline in the terms of trade was 0.5 per annum from 1954 to 1972 and 3.6 per annum from 1973 to 1982. Keynes became particularly preoccupied towards the end of his life with trends and cycles in primary product prices, and I will discuss later his solutions to the problem.

Finally, I turn to what I consider to be the dismal role played by the International Monetary Fund (IMF) in developing countries, which through the pursuit of inappropriate policies based on misleading economic theory has exerted a depressive effect on economic activity in these countries. Because the IMF is a fund, and not a bank with the power to create international money for collectively agreed purposes, it can only lend what it borrows, and as a condition for finance and balance-of-payments support it has always insisted on rapid adjustment within the countries to repay loans in the shortest possible time. Balance-of-payments deficits in turn have always been associated in the IMF's mind with distorted relative prices and excessive aggregate demand which has then led to the standard IMF adjustment package of devaluation and deflation – a recipe for stagflation. The IMF has rarely recognised the structural characteristics of developing countries that I mentioned earlier that may make deficits inevitable in the attempt by developing countries to grow, or that because of supply rigidities and demand inelasticities devaluation may be a singularly inappropriate adjustment weapon. Moreover, the Fund has never recognised that free trade in goods and financial transactions may not be optimal for developing countries, and yet trade and financial liberalisation are invariably conditions for loan support. *Laissez-*

faire and free trade is, as the German Chancellor, Bismarck, once remarked, 'a policy for the strong'. At the same time, pressure has rarely been put on countries with the counterpart surpluses to expand their economies or to revalue their currencies which would help the deficit countries without deflation. In short, the IMF exerts deflationary bias in the world economy through its asymmetrical treatment of deficit and surplus countries. This is not what Keynes envisaged. In the early drafts of his scheme for an International Clearing Union, surplus, as well deficit, countries would have been penalised in a number of ways including the payment of interest on credit balances; the transfer of credit balances to a Reserve Fund; and the obligation to revalue the currency (Kahn, 1976).

KEYNES AND LONG-RUN DEVELOPMENT

Keynes's name is not normally associated with the theory of the long run; with long-run equilibrium, or the process of economic development. We think of Keynesian theory as short-run static analysis associated with the *General Theory*, and with a slightly anglo-centric bias at that. Joseph Schumpeter once remarked:

> practical Keynesianism is a seedling which cannot be transplanted into foreign soil; it dies there and becomes poisonous before it dies. But . . . left in English soil, this seedling is a healthy thing and promises both fruit and shade. Let me say once and for all: all this applies to every bit of advice that Keynes offered. (Schumpeter, 1947, p. 86)

Schumpeter was jealous of Keynes as Kahn makes clear in his recent book *The Making of Keynes' General Theory* (1984) where he describes as absurd Schumpeter's suggestion (Schumpeter, 1954, p. 1172) that his (Kahn's) 'share in the historic achievement (of the *General Theory*) cannot have fallen very far short of co-authorship'. There was, in any case, more than one Keynes. There was Keynes the academic and author of the *General Theory* (which itself is not devoid of insights into the process of long-run development); there was Keynes of the India Office and author of *Indian Currency and Finance*; there was Keynes the essayist and polemicist, and Keynes the *homme d'affaires* and international civil servant who spent a great deal of his working life, particularly in periods of domestic and international crisis, devising schemes to make the world a better place. It is clear from many of his essays and memoranda that Keynes did have a vision of the mainsprings of long-run economic progress at a time when very few, if any, economists were writing about growth and development, and before the sub-discipline of development economics had ever been born. The role of capital accumulation and planning are central themes that run through much of his writings. Also the new aggregate economics of the static *General Theory* gave Roy Harrod, Joan Robinson, Nicholas Kaldor and others the necessary tools to extend Keynesian theory in the long run to provide a framework for the analysis of long-run growth in both developed and developing countries. I shall, however, take away some credit from Harrod by arguing that Keynes in his essay on 'Some Economic Consequences of a Declining Population' (1937) actually anticipated Harrod's 'An Essay in Dynamic Theory' (1939), and that it was Keynes who invented the concepts of the warranted and natural growth rates which provide the analytical framework for the discussion of so much economic policy in developing countries, particularly policies to raise the savings ratio; the quest for techniques of production to reduce the capital:output ratio, and policies to control population.[3] Finally, in his later years Keynes saw clearly the world as an inter-dependant system linked together through trade where balance-of-payments problems in some countries and primary product price fluctuations may impair the functioning of the whole world economy. It was therefore imperative, he thought, to have institutional mechanisms to take deflationary bias out of the world economy and to stabilise primary product prices. These matters are as relevant to developing countries today as they were when Keynes was writing about them in the late 1930s and early 1940s.

CAPITAL ACCUMULATION

If we go back to Keynesian fundamentals, what drives a capitalist economy is the decision to invest and the rate of capital accumulation. The rate of accumulation is governed by decisions to invest, not by decisions to save. This is a fundamental difference between Keynesian and pre-Keynesian thinking. The process of economic development may be described as a generalised process of capital accumulation, and developing countries may be characterised as capital scarce. There is a strong association across countries between the level of capital deepening and income per head and between the ratio of investment to GDP and the rate of growth of output (Sen, 1983). Crucial to the investment decision is an ample supply of dynamic entrepreneurs willing to take risks. Keynes remarks in the *General Theory* (p. 150): 'if human nature felt no temptation to take a chance, no satisfaction (profit apart) in constructing a factory, a railway, a mine or a farm, there might not be much investment merely as a result of cold calculation'. He goes on:

> Most, probably, of our decisions to do something positive, the full consequences of which will be drawn out over many days to come, can only be taken as a result of animal spirits – of a spontaneous urge to action rather than inaction, and not as the outcome of a weighted average of quantitative benefits multiplied by quantitative probabilities. Enterprise only pretends to itself to be mainly actuated by the statements in its own prospectus, however candid and sincere. Only a little more than an expedition to the South Pole, is it based on an exact calculation of benefits to come. Thus if animal spirits are dimmed and the spontaneous optimism falters, leaving us to depend on nothing but a mathematical expectation, enterprise will fade and die; – though fears of loss may have a basis no more reasonable than hopes of profit had before. (p. 161)

With the emphasis on investment and risk taking, Keynes is

assigning to the entrepreneur the same role as Schumpeter (1943) in his theory of economic development based on the process of 'creative destruction'. What if animal spirits are dimmed and the urge to accumulate is weak? In the context of the developed countries in the 1930s, his position was quite clear; the government must act:

> I expect to see the State, which is in a position to calculate the marginal efficiency of capital goods on long views and on the basis of the general social advantage, taking an ever greater responsibility for directly organising investment . . . The State will have to exercise a guiding influence on the propensity to consume, partly through its scheme of taxation, partly by fixing the rate of interest, and partly, perhaps, in other ways.
> (*General Theory*, p. 378)

It is interesting to speculate what he thought those other ways might be especially in considering poor countries where the powers of governments to tax and to fix the appropriate rate of interest are much weaker. He may have had in mind inflationary finance and forced saving.

In his *A Tract on Monetary Reform* (1923) Keynes described inflation as 'a form of taxation that the public finds hard to evade and even the weakest government can enforce when it can enforce nothing else', Keynes recognised in both the *Treatise on Money* (1930) and *Essays in Persuasion* (1931) that the price of financial conservatism may be economic stagnation. In the *Treatise* he remarks on the extraordinary correspondence in history between periods of inflation and deflation and national rise and decline, respectively:

> in what degree [did] the greatness of Athens [depend] on the silver mines of Laurium – not because the monetary metals are more truly wealth than other things, but because by their effect on prices they supply the spur of profit? . . . [was it] coincidence that the decline and fall of Rome was contemporaneous with the most prolonged and drastic deflation yet

recorded?; [and whether] if the long stagnation of the Middle Ages may not have been more surely and inevitably caused by Europe's meagre supply of the monetary metals than by monasticism or Gothic frenzy? (p. 150)

In *Essays in Persuasion* he described inflation as unjust and deflation as inexpedient but of the two inflation is to be preferred because 'it is worse in an impoverished world to provoke unemployment than to disappoint the rentier'. He recognised that inflation to raise the rate of capital accumulation may have regressive distributional consequences, but argued that the long-run gains to the wage earners can outweigh the short term losses:

> the working class may benefit far more in the long run from the forced abstinence which a profit inflation imposes on them than they lose in the first instance in the shape of diminished consumption so long as wealth and its fruits are not consumed by the nominal owner but are accumulated. (Keynes, 1930)

Keynes's first explicit excursion into the realm of long-run analysis was his 1930 essay on 'The Economic Possibilities of Our Grandchildren' (Keynes, 1931) where he lays down four conditions for economic progress: the power to control population; the determination to avoid wars and civil dissensions; the willingness to entrust to science the direction of those matters which are properly the concern of science; and the rate of accumulation as fixed by the margin between our production and our consumption. The primacy of the investment decision is paramount. Mankind's slow material progress up to 1700 AD resulted from a paucity of technical improvements and very little capital accumulation. He attributes the start of material progress in the modern age to rising prices and profit inflation resulting from the silver and gold discoveries in the New World. The power of accumulation by compound interest then took over, and the power of compound interest over 200 years is such as to 'stagger the imagination'. He recalls how Drake plundered Spanish treasures in 1580, which Queen Elizabeth partly used to pay off England's foreign debt and to balance the budget, and then invested £40,000 in the Levant Company, the profits from which were used to finance the East India Company and which became the foundation of England's foreign investment. Keynes notes that £40,000 accumulating at 3.25 per cent per annum gave the current value of Britain's foreign investment of £4000 million. 'Every £1 Drake brought home in 1580 has now become £100,000. Such is the power of compound interest.' On the basis of the power of compound interest he predicted that the standard of living in progressive countries one hundred years hence would be between four and eight times higher than in 1930. From this he concludes that

> assuming no important wars and no important increases in population, the economic problem may be solved, or be at least within reach of solution, within a hundred years. This means that the economic problem is not – if we look into the future – the permanent problem of the human race.

Economic forecasting is a hazardous occupation, and another fifty years is a long time to wait for validation of Keynes's prediction, but he may well be right for most countries of the world (as our earlier calculations suggest) in the sense that productivity will be high enough to free mankind from the necessity of continuous work merely to subsist.

POPULATION AND CAPITAL ACCUMULATION

Developing countries may be characterised as countries where the natural rate of growth exceeds the warranted rate of growth; that is, where the growth of population and labour productivity exceeds the rate of capital accumulation (Thirlwall, 1974). Keynes invented this framework, although not the terminology. There are many disadvantages of rapid population growth, but

lso advantages if the warranted rate of growth exceeds the
natural rate. In the late 1930s Keynes became worried that the
rate of population growth, which was slowing down in England
and other developed countries, would not be sufficient to induce
capitalists to invest enough to absorb full employment saving,
which would ultimately lead to stagnation. Yet he fully
recognised the Malthusian worry of excessive population growth
on living standards and human welfare, a topic on which he had
expressed views much earlier in his life. In 1921 the editor of the
Manchester Guardian had asked Keynes to be general editor of a
series of special supplements on the financial and economic
problems of post-war Europe. In a general introduction to the
Reconstruction of Europe series for the second number of the supplements he asserts that the basic answer to the world's
economic and political problems lies in 'the principles of
pacificism and population or birth control', 'the prolegomena to
any future scheme of social improvement' as he describes it.
Specifically on population he remarks

> indeed the problem of population is going to be not merely an
> economists' problem, but in the near future the greatest of all
> political questions. It will be a question which will arouse
> some of the deepest instincts and emotions of men, and
> feelings may run as passionately as in earlier struggles between
> religions. (Johnson, 1977, p. 440)

Keynes expressed his worry about a falling rate of population
growth in a lecture to the Eugenics Society in 1937 (Keynes,
1937).[4] Consider a society with a savings ratio of 8–15 per cent
and a capital-output ratio of 4 giving a rate of capital accumulation which will absorb saving of 2–4 per cent. With a constant
capital:output ratio this is also the required growth rate. Can this
growth rate be guaranteed? Historically it appeared to Keynes
that one-half of the increase in capital accumulation could be
attributed to increased population; the other half to increased
living standards (with the capital:output ratio roughly constant).
Now suppose population growth falls to zero. Since the standard

of life cannot be expected to grow by more than one per cent, this means that the demand for capital will grow at only one per cent while the supply grows at between 2–4 per cent – a clear and worrying imbalance which would have to be rectified either by reducing saving or reducing the rate of interest to lengthen the average period of production (i.e. to raise the capital:output ratio).[5] Economists should immediately recognise this discussion as exactly analogous to Harrod's discussion of divergences between the warranted and natural rates of growth (Harrod, 1939; 1948). The required rate of growth to absorb saving (the savings ratio divided by the required incremental capital:output ratio) is the warranted rate of growth and the actual growth determined by population and rising living standards (productivity growth through technical progress) is the natural rate of growth. Harrod's dynamic theory is precisely anticipated by Keynes.[6]

Keynes is cleary ambivalent on the question of the relation between population growth and economic development, as I am (Thirlwall, 1985). He agrees with Malthus that a stationary population facilitates a rising standard of life, but only on condition that the resources released are utilised:

> for we have now learned that we have another devil at our elbow at least as fierce as the Malthusian – namely the devil of unemployment escaping through the breakdown of effective demand. Perhaps we could call this devil too a Malthusian devil since it was Malthus himself who first told us about him. . . Now when Malthusian devil P is chained up, Malthusian devil U is likely to break loose. When devil P of population is chained up, we are free of one menace; but we are more exposed to the other devil U of unemployed resources than we were before.

Keynes's concern is probably not applicable to most developing countries today where population growth is still rapid and where the natural rate of growth exceeds the warranted rate. However, the framework of analysis which Keynes devised is extremely useful for analysing the coexistence of unemployment and inflationary pressure in capital scarce countries, and secular stagnation in capital abundant countries, as Harrod later did more extensively. The Keynes–Harrod framework has also subsequently been widely used for the planning of investment requirements for growth in developing countries.

THE TERMS OF TRADE AND DEFLATIONARY BIAS

I now turn to matters more international in scope and to one of the depressive factors that I mentioned earlier which affects poor countries; namely, the terms of trade of primary commodities. The developing countries in particular, and the world economy in general, suffer several problems from the uncontrolled movements of primary commodity prices. First, there is the fact mentioned at the beginning of the gradual trend deterioration in the prices of primary commodities relative to industrial goods which reduces the real income and welfare of the developing countries directly. Secondly, primary product prices are much more cyclically volatile than industrial goods' prices. My own research shows that over the period 1960 to 1982, the elasticity of prices of primary products exported by developing countries with respect to the prices of industrial goods was 2.4. Disaggregation by commodity group shows an elasticity of 1.25 for food; 1.3 for agricultural non-food products, and 2.9 for minerals including petroleum (Thirlwall and Bergevin, 1985). This volatility has a number of detrimental consequences. First, it leads to a great deal of instability in the foreign exchange earnings and balance of payments position of developing countries which makes investment planning and economic management much more difficult than otherwise would be the case. Secondly, because of asymmetries in the economic system, volatility imparts inflationary bias combined with tendencies to depression in the world economy at large. When primary product prices fall, the demand for industrial goods falls but their prices are sticky downwards. When primary product prices rise, industrial goods prices are quick to follow suit and governments depress demand to control inflation. The result is stagflation (Kaldor, 1976). Thirdly, the volatility of primary product prices leads to volatility in the terms of trade which may not reflect movements in the equilibrium terms of trade between primary products and industrial goods in the sense that supply and demand are equated in both markets. In these circumstances world economic growth becomes either supply constrained if primary product prices are 'too high', or demand constrained if primary product prices are 'too low' (Kaldor, 1976; Thirlwall, 1986). On all these macroeconomic grounds there is a *prima facie* case for attempting to introduce a greater degree of stability into markets for primary commodities including, I believe, oil.[7] Keynes was very much concerned with this issue both during, and in the years immediately preceding, the Second World War. In a memorandum in 1942 on the 'International Regulation of Primary Commodities' he remarks that 'one of the greatest evils in international trade before the war was the wide and rapid fluctuations in the world price of primary commodities . . . It must be the primary purpose of control to prevent these wide fluctuations' (Moggridge, 1980). However, Keynes first addressed himself to this matter in a serious way in 1938 in a paper read before the British Association and subsequently published in the *Economic Journal* entitled 'The Policy of Government Storage of Foodstuffs and Raw Materials'. He noted that for the four commodities of rubber, cotton, wheat and lead, the price had fluctuated by 67 per cent in the previous ten years, and was led to remark 'assuredly nothing can be more inefficient than the present system by which the price is always too high or too low and there are frequent meaningless fluctuations in the plant and labour force employed'. He blamed the state of affairs on insufficient incentives in the competitive system for the individual enterprise to store surplus stocks of materials because stocks yield a negative return in terms of themselves. The government had just passed the Essential Commodities Reserve Act with the object of accumulating stocks of commodities for use in war time. The intention was for government to purchase stock and to attempt to increase stocks physically held in the country by other sources. The Act contained wide powers for the provision or subsidy of storage and for finance to induce traders to hold above normal stocks, and Keynes saw their potential for use in peace as well as war. He reflected: 'if only we could tackle the problem of peace with the same energy and wholeheartedness as we tackle those of war', but expressed optimism that 'it may be possible, as I hope to show it is, to combine the primary object of the Government's new Act with purposes useful in peace'. His proposal was that the government should offer storage to all Empire producers of specified raw materials, either free of warehouse charges and interest or a nominal charge, provided they ship the surplus to approved warehouses. The government might even offer interest-free finance up to 98 per cent of the market price at the date of delivery into storage. Keynes saw several advantages to the plan. First, the cost to the Treasury would be small in relation to the volume of resources involved, giving much greater security for a modest outlay. £500 million of commodities might be held for a cost of £20 million. Secondly, the moderation of price fluctuations would ensure a more continuous scale of output in the producing countries:

> in war such reserves held in this country would be better than a gold mine; in peace we might find that we had taken the first step forwards making possible a steadier scale of output of the principal raw materials, and thus avoiding extreme fluctuations of demand for our own exports from the raw material countries.

There is explicit recognition here of the mutual interdependence of developed and developing countries; the major theme of the Brandt Report which Mr Heath will discuss later. Thirdly, Keynes recognised that finance might pose some problem for the exchanges, but argued that it could be regarded as a form of foreign investment 'the security for which would offer the great advantage of being situated at home'. Moreover, it would be a once-for-all transaction up to the value of the stocks to be held. There would be no interest, but it would still be worthwhile to forego the cash income of £20 million a year in return for the compensating advantages of greater security, a stimulus to the export industries, an increased control over the trade cycle and an insurance against having to pay excessive prices at a later date.

Keynes followed up his observations and proposals with a more detailed plan in 1942 for what he called 'commod control,' an international body representing leading producers and consumers that would stand ready to buy 'commods' (Keynes's name for typical commodities), and store them, at a price (say) 10 per cent below the fixed basic price and sell them at 10 per cent above (Moggridge, 1980). The basic price would have to be adjusted according to whether there was a gradual run-down or build-up of stocks, indicating that the price is either 'too low' or 'too high'. If production did not adjust (at least downwards), Keynes recognised that production quotas might have to be implemented although in general he was of the view that commodity policy should be more concerned with stabilisation than restriction. Commodities should be stored as widely as possible across producing and consuming centres. This proposal is of some contemporary relevance at a time when close to 100 million people in the world are currently the victims of famine, not because the world is short of food, or these events cannot be foreseen, but because of a political paralysis which prevents the world from organising itself in anticipation of such disasters. One solution would be to have a system of granaries strategically placed across the world under international supervision which could store the surpluses of the 'north' and release them at a time of need. This in no way need preclude or hinder the fundamental agricultural reforms that everyone recognises are necessary in many of the famine-ridden countries of Africa if there is to be self-sustaining growth. In Keynes's scheme, finance for the storage and holding of 'commods' would have been provided through his proposal for an International Clearing Union, acting like a world Central Bank, with which 'commod controls' would keep accounts.[8] At the present time, finance for storage and holding could be provided through the issue of Special Drawing Rights (SDRs) by the IMF. Keynes believed, with some justification, that such a 'commod control' scheme would make a major contribution to curing the international trade cycle. Indeed, the injection and withdrawal of purchasing power by buying up 'commods' when prices are falling and selling them when prices are rising would operate much more immediately and effectively than public works. Keynes remarked

> at present, a falling off in effective demand in the industrial consuming countries causes a price collapse which means a corresponding break in the level of incomes and of effective demand in the raw material producing centres, with a further adverse reaction, by repercussion, on effective demand in the industrial centres; and so, in the familiar way, the slump proceeds from bad to worse. And when the recovery comes, the rebound to excessive demands through the stimulus of inflated price promotes, in the same evil manner, the excesses of the boom. (Moggridge, 1980, p. 121)

Kanbur and Vines have shown in a recent paper (1984) that the income multiplier is four times larger when the terms of trade oscillate procyclically than when the terms of trade are assumed fixed.

After substantial criticisms and redrafting, the Official Committee on Post-War External Problems finally sent Keynes's plan to the War Cabinet. James Meade tells the story that when Churchill got wind of the scheme for buffer stocks he was overheard in casual conversation to remark 'what's all this I hear about butter scotch'! (Worswick and Trevithick, 1983, p. 132). Ultimately, the plan was not adopted because of opposition from the Bank of England and the Ministry of Agriculture for different reasons.[9] Over forty years on from Keynes's war-time proposal, primary product price fluctuations still plague the world economy. The world still lacks the requisite international mechanisms to rectify what is a major source of instability for the world economy leading to inflation and depression. From 1980–84, for example, primary product prices fell on average by 24 per cent, and this was a major cause of the international debt crisis in 1983 which still lingers. UNCTAD's proposal for an Integrated

Programme for Commodities has not been successful. The IMF's Compensatory Finance Scheme and Stabex established by the Lomé Convention, which compensate poor countries for shortfalls in export earnings below trend, are welcome, but they represent a drop in the ocean, and do not get to the crux of the problem of price instability.

Apart from fluctuations in primary product prices, there are many other sources of deflationary bias in the world economy which Keynes was aware of and was seeking to avoid in his proposals for an International Clearing Union. They include: protectionism and beggar-thy-neighbour policies because of inadequate finance to sustain balance of payments deficits; continual pressure on deficit countries to adjust without symmetrical pressure on surplus countries to expand or revalue their currencies; structural deficits and surpluses arising from the dissimilar and unequal economic structures of rich and poor countries; inadequate financial institutions to channel funds from surplus countries to deficit countries most in need, and the lack of a truly international money to bring together countries which desperately need resources with those who have spare resources and willing to export more. In the second Keynes Seminar (Thirlwall, 1976), Lord Kahn outlined in intricate detail the historical origins of the IMF and the difference between the Keynes Plan for an International Clearing Union and the IMF which ultimately emerged at Bretton Woods (Kahn, 1976), and John Williamson will tell us later how he thinks the world would have fared and functioned had the Keynes plan been adopted at Bretton Woods rather than the White Plan. Suffice it to say here that the Clearing Union would have been based on a new international bank money, Bancor, fixed in terms of gold. The Central Banks of all member countries would have kept accounts with the Clearing Union through which they would have settled balances with each other at par values defined in terms of Bancor. Countries with persistent credit balances would have been penalised just as heavily as those with debit balances. Countries would have been charged one per cent per annum on the amount of their average credit or debit balance in Bancor in excess of a quarter of their quota subscription to the Union, and a further one per cent on their average credit or debit balance in excess of one-half their quota. If credit balances exceeded 50 per cent of quota on the average of at least one year, the country would have to discuss with the Governing Board appropriate measures to restore equilibrium.[10] Today we not only lack institutional mechanisms to stabilise primary product prices, but there is no institutional pressure on surplus countries, no international money to serve the needs of the developing countries, and the principle of the scarce currency clause that recognised protection against surplus countries as a legitimate (welfare creating) form of protection has never been resurrected.

CONCLUSION

In this paper I have tried to set the scene for the rest of the Seminar by discussing some of the economic forces that impede the progress of poor countries and depress the functioning of the world economy, showing that Keynes was also interested in many of the issues which development economists are concerned with today. This is not surprising since Keynes always approached his economics from a practical point of view, seeking to throw theoretical light on pressing contemporary problems and then devising schemes and institutional structures for their solution. He treated economics as essentially a branch of ethics, in the Marshallian tradition. Indeed, he once described what drew him to economics. It was, he said, its combination of the practical and mathematical coupled with its potentiality for good. What better reason for studying economics, particularly development economics: the challenge is immense.

ACKNOWLEDGEMENTS

I am grateful to Brian Reddaway, Lesley Pressnell, Charles Kennedy, Bob Dixon and Jan Kregel for helpful comments on an early draft of this paper.

APPENDIX: KEYNES AND INDIA

(This appendix relies heavily on two books: Keynes's own book *Indian Currency and Finance* (1913), and Vol. XV of the *Collected Writings of John Maynard Keynes, Activities 1906–1914 India and Cambridge* (Johnson, 1971). See also Chandavarkar (1983).)

Keynes entered the India Office in October 1906, having placed second in the Civil Service examinations to Otto Niemeyer, who chose the Treasury. Initially he was a junior clerk in the Military Department, and then in March 1907 he was switched to the Revenue Statistics and Commerce Department. He resigned two years later on his 25th Birthday (5 June) to take up a lectureship in economics at Cambridge financed by the 'Prof' (A.C. Pigou). In 1909, Keynes's first major article appeared in the March *Economic Journal* on 'Recent Economic Events in India'. This was an analysis of the recent inflation in India, the prices of exports and principal articles consumed having risen by over 40 per cent between 1903 and 1907 (compared with only 16 per cent in the United Kingdom). He adopted a basically 'quantity theory' explanation, noting the close correspondence between the rise in prices and the quantity of money in circulation which also rose by just over 40 per cent. Keynes attributed the increase in the money supply to an inflow of foreign capital, which aroused some interest since it was believed at the time that India was experiencing a capital outflow. Keynes never visited India, but his two years in the India Office, although boring for him, had clearly sparked his interest in Indian affairs and particularly in the peculiarities and intricacies of its monetary arrangements. Alfred Marshall, Keynes's mentor, had a similar interest since his early lecturing days in Oxford, and had given evidence in 1899 to the Indian Currency Committee (the Fowler Commission). After his departure from the India Office, Keynes continued to review various documents produced by the Office, and in 1909 he was involved in lengthy correspondence in the columns of *The Economist* newspaper on the size of foreign investments in India. At this period of his life, Keynes was a committed free trader, and in 1910 he addressed the Indian undergraduate debating society in Cambridge (the Majlis) on the theme of India and Protection.

In May 1910, Keynes was asked to give six lectures at the London School of Economics on Indian finance which he duly delivered under the title of 'Currency, Finance and the Level of Prices in India'. He then read a paper to the Royal Economic Society in May 1911 on the same theme of the Indian Currency Question, which contained the seeds of the ideas which flowered two years later in his book *Indian Currency and Finance*.

Up to 1893, India had been on a silver standard with the gold value of the rupee fluctuating with the gold value of silver bullion. The gold value of silver had been depreciating making the management of the public finances difficult because of the large payments which the Indian government had to make in sterling. In 1893, the value of the rupee was finally divorced from the value of the metal contained in it. In effect, although without conscious decision, the Indian currency had been changed from a silver standard to a gold exchange standard, with the rupee fixed in terms of sterling and sterling fixed in terms of gold. Keynes says in his 1911 paper:

> I will endeavour to give reasons for thinking that this existing system to which the name Gold Exchange Standard has been given, is something much more civilised, much more economical and much more satisfactory than a gold currency. I should like to see it openly established in India on a permanent basis and all talk of an eventual gold currency definitely abandoned... The government of India has been the first to adopt the Gold Exchange Standard on a large scale. But every year there are fresh converts; nor will it be long before it becomes, in effect, the standard of half the world. And out of it, in my belief, will be evolved the ideal currency of the future. (Johnson, 1971, p. 69)

Ricardo at the time of the bullionist controversy had extolled the virtues of a gold exchange standard, arguing that as long as gold is available for payments of international indebtedness at a fixed rate in terms of the national currency, it does not matter what the national currency consists of, so that there can be an enormous resource saving by using a cheap material.

The currency issue was by no means settled, however. The Indian Currency Committee of 1899 had advocated the introduction of a gold currency in India as well as a gold standard. While the latter recommendation was implemented, the former was thwarted, but there continued to be a considerable body of opinion in its favour particularly in view of the rapid rise in prices experienced during the first decade of the century. These sentiments were later to emerge from witnesses to the Royal Commission on Indian Finance and Currency set up in 1913. Keynes in his book made two other telling points against a gold currency. First, not only is the circulation of precious metals wasteful of real resources, but if gold is wanted for export, the internal monetary system is inconvenienced if gold also circulates as a medium of exchange. Secondly, there is the seigniorage aspect of currency arrangements to consider. Keynes noted that during the period 1901 to 1913, the government had been able to accumulate a sum of about £21 million from the profits of the rupee coinage, and the annual income derivable from the interest on the sums set free by the use of cheap forms of currency amounted to about £1 million. The introduction of a gold currency would jeopardise that seigniorage.

The Royal Commission on Indian Finance and Currency, under the Chairmanship of Austen Chamberlain, was established in 1913 against a background of allegations of various forms of corruption rife over the buying and selling of silver for the Indian gold standard reserve. Keynes was initially invited to be Secretary of the Commission, and then a full member. *Indian Currency and Finance* was published in the same year. The terms of reference of the Commission were to study: (a) the management of the balances of the government of India in India, and of the India Office in London; (b) the sale of Council drafts by the Secretary of State in London; (c) the gold standard reserve; the paper currency reserve, and the system by which the exchange value of the rupee was maintained, and (d) the financial organisation and procedures of the India Office.

Keynes saw as one of his major tasks to persuade the rest of the Commission that the direction the Indian Currency had taken towards a gold exchange standard was the right one, and in this he succeeded. The Commission endorsed the gold exchange standard; and there can be no doubt about Keynes's influence on the Commission's Report in general. In a letter to Keynes, Austen Chamberlain admitted: 'I am amazed to see how largely the views of the Commission as disclosed by our informal discussions are a mere repetition of the arguments and conclusions to which your study had previously led you' (Johnson 1971, p. 100). Secondly, Keynes was anxious to promote monetary reform partly to accelerate the monetisation of the Indian economy and partly to improve monetary management by extending the money market and bank rate control, and making money and credit more elastic to the needs of trade. On the question of monetisation of the economy, Keynes had written in 1910: 'in many parts of India, even at the present time, barter exists to a very considerable extent. It must be the principal object of any currency scheme to hasten, so far as possible, what is known as the process of adaeration, or transition from barter to money' (Johnson, 1971, p. 61). To improve monetary management and the 'elasticity' of the currency, Keynes urged the establishment of a central bank supervising the holding of all the country's various reserves:

> with no central reserve, no elasticity of credit currency, hardly a rediscount market, and hardly a bank rate policy, with the growth of small and daring banks, great increase of deposits and a community unhabituated to banking and ready at the least alarm to revert to hoarding . . . there are to be found most elements of weakness and few elements of strength. (Johnson 1971, p. 197)

At the time, the terms of reference of the Commission did not in fact include consideration of the establishment of a central bank, but the Commission neverthless requested that Keynes should prepare a set of proposals. Keynes first commented on a plan for a State Bank drawn up by Sir Lionel Abraham,[11] and then prepared his own memorandum following his brief statement on the need for such a bank in *Indian Currency and Finance*. Keynes's major concern was over the use and management of the country's various reserves. Lacking a central bank the government's cash reserves were held in Reserve Treasuries all over the country mainly in the form of notes. The paper currency reserve provided 100 per cent gold and silver backing for the note issue (with provision for a 20 per cent fiduciary issue). In addition there was the gold standard reserve. Keynes wanted all three reserves to be treated as one big reserve under the control of a central bank to give such a Bank more resource flexibility and a greater ability to expand credit as the need arose, particularly in the busy (harvest) season. Originally the Commission were averse to thinking in this way, but Keynes threatened a note of dissent, and ultimately Chamberlain gave way. Keynes did not succeed, however, in persuading the Commission to include his proposal for a state bank in the body of the Report. Instead, it was published as an Annexe and received approval in the Report. The Report of the Royal Commission was published on the 2 March 1914. The outbreak of war, however, prevented the implementation of any of the Commission's recommendations,[12] and the currency situation in India soon became very different. After the war a Committee on Indian Exchange and Currency was established under Sir Henry Babington Smith to examine the working of the monetary system under new conditions. Keynes was a witness. The value of the rupee had risen from 1/4d to 2/4d by December 1919. Keynes thought the rupee should be fixed at a higher rather than a lower level because Indian prices had not risen as fast as world prices, and with the threat of a further rise in world prices, a higher value of the rupee would help to keep domestic prices down. Keynes suggested 2/-. He did not consider that a high value of the rupee would jeopardise exports because if the value was lower this would only cause labour unrest and demands for higher wages. He remarked

if therefore the rupee were to depreciate, the Indian employer would be able to get his labour and possibly certain of his other products, for a time, below what he really ought to pay and that would encourage him. But personally I believe that it is a very unsound way of giving a temporary stimulus to industry. It is a method by which the employer cheats his employees for a space of time. If he does it on any substantial scale he causes political and social difficulties in the long run which will far outweigh the temporary advantages which he has secured. (Johnson, 1971, p. 288)

Keynes was always very concerned about the internal stability of prices for planning. The Committee reported in 1920, taking Keyness' advice and fixing the rupee at 2/- and its ratio to the gold sovereign at 10:1. As it happened world prices dropped sharply in 1920, and the government was unable to maintain the exchange rate at 2/- per rupee. It dropped to 1/- in 1921, climbing back to 1/6d in 1925.

NOTES

1. I am not sure whether this is entirely accurate since Skidelsky (1983) mentions that shipping ten Ayrshire bulls was the first job he was given at the India Office!
2. I cannot help recalling what Joan Robinson once said, however, that it is better for a country to be exploited than not to be exploited at all!
3. I have never seen this argued in print before, except that Joan Robinson (1964) mentions in a postscript to her model of an expanding economy: "that the first use, in its modern form, of the rate of growth of capital derived from the ratio of saving to income and the ratio of income to capital was made by Keynes in his Galton Lecture" (p. 85). I am grateful to Professor Jan Kregel for drawing this to my attention. It would be interesting to know whether there was any correspondence between Harrod and Keynes on this matter after the 1937 essay.
4. He says 'Business expectations being based much more on present than on prospective demand, an era of increasing population tends to promote optimism, since demand will in general tend to exceed, rather than fall short of, what is hoped for. Moreover, a mistake, resulting in a particular type of capital being in temporary over-supply, is in such conditions

rapidly corrected. But in an era of declining population the opposite is true. Demand tends to be below what is expected and a state of over-supply is less easily corrected. Thus a pessimistic atmosphere may issue; and although at long last pessimism may tend to correct itself through its effect on supply the first result to prosperity of a change-over from an increasing to a declining population may be very disastrous' (p. 14).

5. Keynes seems to have anticipated his conclusions in the *General Theory* itself where in his discussion of the trade cycle he remarked 'if, for example, we pass from a period of increasing population into one of declining population, the characteristic phase of the cycle will be lengthened' (p. 318).

6. Harrod himself later expressed concern over Britain's prospect of a declining population in a wartime pamphlet (Harrod, 1943). He dismissed the argument that smaller numbers would make everybody more prosperous ('if there are fewer producers the cake would be proportionately smaller') and attributes the worldwide increase in unemployment between the wars to the slowdown of population growth: 'Unemployment does not exist because there is no work to be done; it results from a flaw in our system of exchange and distribution.' If population ceases to grow, it is more difficult to find profitable outlets for saving and therefore the greater the chance of unemployment. Reddaway (1939) made a more comprehensive study of the issues and was generally less pessimistic about population decline.

7. I stress macroeconomic grounds because in a recent study of commodity policy, Newbery and Stiglitz (1981) conclude their analysis by saying 'the major result . . . is to question seriously the desirability of price stabilisation schemes, both from the point of view of the producers and of the consumer'. They are primarily concerned with the microeconomic aspects of price stabilisation relating to efficiency and welfare, and give short shrift to the macroeconomic aspects of stabilisation, and yet it is the macroeconomic aspects that may be paramount from a development point of view.

8. It was estimated that to hold one year's stock of wheat, maize, sugar, coffee, cotton, wool, rubber and tin would have cost £950 million at 1942 prices.

9. The Bank of England found the proposals 'to be far too laissez-faire inasmuch as they still allow a place for private trading' which displayed in Keynes's view a 'bias towards rigidly controlled State trading on Russian lines'. Keynes wrote to Richard Hopkins on 15 April 1942: 'I can only plead guilty of aiming at a plan which does take a middle course between unfettered competition and laissez-faire conditions and planned controls which try to freeze commerce into a fixed mould' (Moggridge, 1980, pp. 110–11).

The Minister of Agriculture, Mr Hudson; his Permanent Secretary, Sir John Ferguson, and Sir Frederic Leith-Ross were all opposed, arguing that only output restrictions could solve the problem of commodity surpluses. A guaranteed floor price, as in Keynes's scheme, would encourage production instead of diminishing it.

10. According to Rolf Lüke (1985), Dr Schacht, the architect of Germany's war

time preparations and President of the Reichsbank 1924–30, had a plan in 1929, similar to Keynes's International Clearing Union, that would have consisted of a clearing house involving seven national banks which would have given loans to developing countries to enable them to buy German goods to solve the reparations problem, recognising that it would be self-defeating for Germans to export more to the allies themselves.

11. Sir Lionel Abraham was Financial Secretary and later Under Secretary of State for India, and the Commission's most important witness, being the only person (other than Keynes) who really understood all the issues involved.

12. India did not have a central bank until 1935, with an institutional structure very different to that recommended by Keynes.

REFERENCES

Chandavarkar A.G. (1983), 'Money and Credit 1858-1947', in D. Kumar and M. Desai (eds), *The Cambridge Economic History of India, Vol 2: c. 1757-c. 1970* (Cambridge: Cambridge University Press).

Goulet, D. (1971) *The Cruel Choice: A New Concept on the Theory of Development* (New York: Atheneum).

Harrod, R. (1939) 'An Essay in Dynamic Theory', *Economic Journal*, March, pp. 14–33.

Harrod, R. (1943) *Britain's Future Population*, Oxford Pamphlets on Home Affairs.

Harrod, R.F. (1948) *Towards a Dynamic Economics* (London: Macmillan).

Harrod, R.F. (1951) *The Life of John Maynard Keynes* (London: Macmillan).

Hirschman, A. (1981) 'The Rise and Decline of Development Economics', in *Essays in Trespassing: Economics to Politics and Beyond* (Cambridge: Cambridge University Press).

Johnson, E. (1971) *The Collected Writings of John Maynard Keynes, Vol. XV. Activities 1906-1914 India and Cambridge* (London: Macmillan).

Johnson, E. (1977) *The Collected Writings of J.M. Keynes, Vol. XVII: Activities 1920-1922, Treaty Revision and Reconstruction* (London: Macmillan).

Johnson, H.G. (1978) 'Keynes and Development', in H.G. Johnson and E. Johnson (eds), *The Shadow of Keynes* (Oxford: Basil Blackwell).

Kahn, R. (1976) 'Historical Origins of the International Monetary Fund', in A.P. Thirlwall (ed.), *Keynes and International Monetary Relations* (London: Macmillan).

Kahn, R. (1984) *The Making of Keynes' General Theory* (Cambridge: Cambridge University Press).

Kaldor, N. (1976) 'Inflation and Recession in the World Economy', *Economic Journal*, December, pp. 703–14.

Kanbur, S.M.R. and Vines, D. (1984), North–South Interaction and Commod Control, Discussion Paper No. 8 (London: Centre for Economic Policy Research).

Keynes, J.M. (1909) 'Recent Economic Events in India', *Economic Journal*, March, pp. 51–67.

Keynes, J.M. (1913) *Indian Currency and Finance* (London: Macmillan).

Keynes, J.M. (1922) 'An Economist's View of Population', *Manchester Guardian Commercial*, 11 August, reprinted in *Collected Economics Writings*, Vol. XVII, p. 440.

Keynes, J.M. (1923) *A Tract on Monetary Reform*, (London: Macmillan).

Keynes, J.M. (1930) *Treatise on Money*, Vol. 2 (London: Macmillan).

Keynes, J.M. (1931) *Essays in Persuasion* (London: Macmillan).

Keynes, J.M. (1936) *The General Theory of Employment, Interest and Money* (London: Macmillan).

Keynes, J.M. (1937) 'Some Economic Consequences of a Declining Population', *Eugenics Reviews*, April, pp. 13–17.

Keynes, J.M. (1938) 'The Policy of Government Storage of Foodstuffs and Raw Materials', *Economic Journal*, September, pp. 449–60.

Luke, R. (1985) 'The Schacht and the Keynes Plans', *Banca Nazionale del Lavoro Quarterly Review*, March, pp. 65–76.

Moggridge, D. (ed.) (1980), *The Collected Writings of J.M. Keynes, Vol. XXVII: Activities 1940–1946 Shaping the Post-War World: Employment and Commodities* (London: Macmillan).

Myrdal, G. (1957) *Economic Theory and Underdeveloped Regions* (London: Duckworth).

Newbery, D. and Stiglitz, J. (1981), *The Theory of Commodity Price Stabilisation: A Study in the Economics of Risk* (Oxford: Oxford University Press).

Pack, H. (1982) 'Aggregate Implications of Factor Substitution in Industrial Processes', *Journal of Development Economics*, August, pp. 1–37.

Patel, S.J. (1964) 'The Economic Distance Between Nations: Its Origins, Measurement and Outlook', *Economic Journal*, March, pp. 119–31.

Prebisch, R. (1950) *The Economic Development of Latin America and its Principal Problems*, ECLA (New York: United Nations Department of Economic Affairs).

Reddaway, W.B. (1939) *The Economics of a Declining Population* (London: George Allen & Unwin).

Robinson, Joan (1964), *Collected Economic Papers*, Vol 2 (Oxford: Basil Blackwell)

Schumpeter, J. (1943) *Capitalism, Socialism and Democracy* (London: George Allen & Unwin)

Schumpeter, J. (1947) 'Keynes, the Economist', in S. Harris (ed.), *The New Economics: Keynes's Influence on Theory and Public Policy* (New York: Alfred A. Knopf).

Schumpeter, J. (1954) *History of Economic Analysis* (London: George Allen & Unwin).

Sen, A. (1981) *Poverty and Famines: An Essay on Entitlement and Deprivation* (Oxford: Clarendon Press).

Sen, A. (1983) 'Development: Which Way Now?', *Economic Journal*, December, pp. 745–62.

Sen, A. (1984) *Resources, Values and Development* (Oxford: Basil Blackwell).

Singer, H. (1950) 'The Distribution of Gains Between Investing and Borrowing Countries', *American Economic Review Papers and Proceedings*, May, pp. 473–485.

Singer, H. (1982) 'Terms of Trade Controversy and the Evolution of Soft Financing: Early Years in the UN: 1947–1951', in D. Seers and G. Meier (eds), *Pioneers in Development*, World Bank.

Singer, H. (1984) 'Relevance of Keynes for Developing Countries', *Estudos de Economia*, July–September, pp. 419–37.

Skidelsky, R. (1983) *John Maynard Keynes: Hopes Betrayed 1883–1920* (London: Macmillan).

Spraos, J. (1980) 'The Statistical Debate on the Net Barter Terms of Trade Between Primary Commodities and Manufactures', *Economic Journal*, March, pp. 107–28.

Stewart, F. (1972) *Technology and Underdevelopment* (London: Macmillan).

Thirlwall, A.P. (1974) *Inflation, Saving and Growth in Developing Economies* (London: Macmillan).

Thirlwall, A.P. (1976) *Keynes and International Monetary Relations* (London: Macmillan).

Thirlwall, A.P. and Bergevin, J. (1985) 'Trends, Cycles and Asymmetries in Terms of Trade of Primary Commodities from Developed and Less Developed Countries', *World Development*, July, pp. 805–17.

Thirlwall, A.P. (1985) 'Population and Economic Development', *Eugenics Review*, forthcoming.

Thirlwall, A.P. (1986) 'A General Model of Growth and Development on Kaldorian Lines', *Oxford Economic Papers*, June.

Triffin, R. (1960) *Gold and the Dollar Crisis* (New Haven, Conn.: Yale University Press).

Williamson, J. (1983) 'Keynes and the International Economic Order', in D. Worswick and J. Trevithick (eds), *Keynes and the Modern World* (Cambridge: Cambridge University Press).

World Development Report (1985) (Oxford: Oxford University Press).

Worswick, D. and Trevithick, J. (eds) (1983) *Keynes and the Modern World* (Cambridge: Cambridge University Press).

SOME REFLECTIONS BY A KEYNESIAN ECONOMIST ON THE PROBLEMS OF DEVELOPING COUNTRIES
W.B. Reddaway

1. INTRODUCTION: 'KEYNESIAN IDEAS'

'Keynesian ideas' which are relevant to developing countries are far wider than those associated, usually in a rather pejorative sense, with 'Keynesianism' in much current discussion: this seems sometimes to confine Keynesianism to a simple-minded view that a country can 'spend its way out of a depression', without any need to consider carefully the things on which the money is spent or the need for other accompanying action, and without regard to the fact that it is not a closed system.

I shall have something to say about 'demand management' in the course of the paper, though not always by that title: even within that narrow sphere it is well to remember that Keynes was not always concerned with *increasing* demand – he wrote 'How to Pay for the War', as well as 'The Means to Prosperity', and it is the former (with 'the War' replaced by 'Development Expenditures') which is closer to the problems of many developing countries.

Many other aspects of Keynes' work and writings, however, are also highly relevant to the problems of developing countries. His contribution to the work at Bretton Woods is an obvious case in point. Whatever developing countries may think and say about the IMF, with its emphasis on short-term finance and on the adoption of deflationary policies which will enable the borrowing country to repay, they have clearly benefited from the long-term loans supplied by the World Bank: they have special reason to appreciate the fact that the Bank developed a system of ultra-soft fifty-year 'credits' through the International Development Association, to be made to poor countries which

36

were unlikely to be able to repay the normal Bank loans.[1] The idea that Keynesian ideas dealt only with the position of a closed system is clearly absurd: the 'Tract on Monetary Reform', the 'transfer' problem and many other writings prove this, and some of the ideas are directly relevant to less-developed countries' problems.

One needs also to consider the work which Keynes did on the whole topic of investment, and its dependence on the expectations of entrepreneurs: these should, in principle, be based on a careful assessment of the long-term future, but such assessments are bound to be very uncertain, so that decisions tend to be over-influenced by the current position (which is more or less known, though frequently of little relevance) and the vagaries of 'animal spirits'. This is clearly relevant to the case for governments of developing countries taking special action in relation to the distribution of capital expenditure, as well as its total amount, especially if there is a plan to change a country's pattern of activities (on this, much more below).

Finally, there is one 'Keynesian idea' to which I subscribe heartily, and which is highly relevant to developing countries. The object of economic analysis is not simply to understand rather better how an economy works (or stagnates), but to provide a basis for action to improve it.

Two corollaries to this idea seem to me of the utmost importance:

(a) It is futile for a government to confine its investment activities to cases where success is absolutely assured: we live in a world of economic uncertainty, especially about the long-term future, and the '100 per cent assurance' (or even 95 per cent) would have to rest on assumptions, which may not prove justified. The hypothesised 'rule' would simply be a formula for complete inactivity.[2]

(b) On the other hand, intervention in current operations (e.g. in the distribution of fertiliser) cannot be justified simply by showing defects in the existing system, which could in principle be reduced or eliminated by control or nationalisation. One needs to feel assured that there would *in practice* be improvements, after allowing for lack of proper data to those running an 'administered' system, and for human shortcomings.

2. PLAN OF THIS PAPER

I have found it surprisingly difficult to devise a logical plan for a paper with the title originally agreed 'The Relevance of Keynesian Ideas in Developing Countries'. If a developing country had a number of discrete problems, and each of these was to be tackled by a separate remedy which had no other effects, then it would not, in logic, be too difficult to consider what sorts of basic ideas were most fruitful in suggesting good remedies for the problems, or perhaps to say which types of problem were best tackled from one approach, and which from another. Even so, there would probably be many cases where two approaches suggested the same action: and with Keynes having produced so many different ideas, which overlap with another peoples' treatment, any scoring system would be difficult to apply.

In point of fact, however, the position of developing countries is better represented by the idea that they have a package of interrelated problems, which need to be tackled by a package of interrelated remedies, and these remedies may be regarded as derived from a number of different thinkers: I am personally quite incapable of saying who deserves priority for the production of some idea, which may have several more-or-less independent originators, and which has not become a part of the common tool-kit – often with many variations and/or improvements added to the original idea.

The editor kindly agreed to a change of title which enabled me to adopt a procedure which follows the principle of comparative advantage, that is to concentrate on development matters about which I have derived some knowledge from my work in developing countries, and which seem to be of real importance: my treatment therefore reflects mainly experience in India, Bangladesh, the Middle East, Nigeria and Ghana, but with some ideas from Latin American countries where I have spent less time. I claim no originality for the ideas which have become part of my stock-in-trade; nor do I wish to label any of them as specifically Keynesian or to attribute them to anybody else. Because they have been gradually assimilated, largely 'on the job', I do not know their exact origin, and to avoid unfairness in attribution I shall make no references to works by other authors – though obviously this does not deny their importance. One of the major themes which I shall seek to emphasise is 'interconnections', in particular the interconnection between theories about investment and the 'practical' points which arise in the implementation of investment programmes and projects.

More specifically, I shall start by reviewing very briefly the 'typical' character of developing countries (so far as generalisations seem useful) and the nature of their main objectives and problems. These differ, at least in degree and relative importance, from those found in developed countries, and I shall consider very briefly some of the ways in which this calls for different economic tools (as opposed to the use of the same tools in different ways, or with different relative frequency).

I shall then discuss, with illustrations, the important points of strategy and methods of application. A good deal of the emphasis will be on problems of application, which are not much covered by Keynesian ideas. People can draw their own conclusions about the importance of the latter.

Finally, I should perhaps 'declare my position', so that people can be on their guard against biases. I class myself as a Keynesian, though I am willing to adopt what seem to be good ideas from any source; Keynes was my supervisor at Cambridge, and I got my first two jobs on the strength of his recommendations. But in my work in developing countries I have found that common sense points on administration and the like have been more valuable than economic theory, even though the latter (on essentially Keynesian lines) doubtless provided an essential foundation.

3. DEVELOPING COUNTRIES AND THEIR PROBLEMS

(i) At the Aggregate Level

Developing countries are a very varied lot, and in many ways need to be studied in sub-groups, or even one at a time, before the analysis can be meaningful. One almost universal feature, which is virtually part of the definition, is that they have a low level of real national income per head. 'Lowness' is judged by reference to the position in developed countries, and this inevitably means that there are borderline problems:[3] *natura non facit saltum* is as true in this field as in other parts of economics, but this does not inhibit useful analysis.

This low level of real income per head is nearly always associated with a low level of real capital per head (including usable land): this seems to be a root cause of the low income level, although one can point to many other contributory forces in many countries, e.g. poor 'organisation' in the widest sense (including law and order) and low levels of skills. It may on occasion be that a higher level of real demand would enable the country to increase its output significantly: but in the main the trouble is the low level of its (present) potential, not a failure to make use of the potential which it already has. In this sense the problem is quite different from the one which the narrow version of Keynesianism is supposed to tackle. The basic problem is to raise the level of potential output: of course it will also be necessary to ensure that this potential is properly used, but that side of the problem is almost 'taken as read'.

The usual 'solution' is seen in terms of raising the stock of real capital faster than population increases. This is essentially a *long-term process*, not one to be achieved in the year or two, which one associates with slump removal in developed countries. Moreover, the literature rightly puts much emphasis on the 'poverty trap': a country with a low level of income per head cannot easily save much to build up its physical capital. Hence the case for the injection of external capital, whether as a gift, or a long-term loan, or direct investment. It used to be fashionable to hope that this will get the developing country over the initial hump and onto a process of self-sustaining growth: such hopes are less fashionable now, but good measures to secure capital inflows (on which Keynesian ideas are clearly relevant) can play an important role.

A number of points need to be added to this conventional analysis, even before we leave the level of aggregates and descend to the nitty-gritty analysis in disaggregated terms:

(a) The first is the traditional – and very important – point that the level of capital per head can be raised much faster if the growth of population (a traditional feature of developing countries) is slowed down. This is a matter on which a generalist external adviser should always stress its importance, but should not (in my view) get involved in details. As a tourist in China I was, however, fascinated by the drastic rules which limit most parents to a one-child family, as a means of changing the trend.

(b) It is all too often true in developing countries that the output obtained from a given stock of capital is far lower than it should be. This takes many forms: too many lorries are off the roads for lack of repair facilities, skills or spare parts; machinery is carelessly used and under-maintained; multiple shifts (which directly raise the weekly output from a given stock of capital, even if working methods are unchanged) are used much less frequently than they might be; essential raw materials, power and the like are inadequate; 'lack of orders' for specific products leads to cutbacks.[4] Hence measures to secure a better use of existing capital – which may or may not mean additional direct employment – can be an invaluable complement to increases in capital, and can produce results more quickly and at less cost.

(c) Better education and better 'organisation' of many kinds (including transport facilities) may do much to raise output without formally increasing the stock of physical capital. A special case, mentioned because it is important, is the introduction of better agricultural practices, high-lighted by the so-called 'green revolution'. Sometimes these involve extra capital, but the gain in output (e.g. from better seeds) can be quite disproportionate, and it would be misleading to attribute the extra output simply to the extra capital.[5]

(d) The relationship between national saving and national income does not have to be treated as given, even in a poor country. Good public finance (including good methods of tax collection) can increase *government* saving directly; that and other devices can also stimulate private saving, as well as better use of these savings (productive capital, not gold bangles).

(e) Finally, of course, one wants current demand management to be good enough to avoid current savings from being reduced by a slump – or by wild inflation.

(ii) Disaggregated Analysis

All these problems become both more complicated and more meaningful if one pursues the analysis simultaneously on an aggregated and a disaggregated level. Even the simple idea of raising the level of income per head by securing more capital clearly requires consideration of the *type* of physical assets to be installed: it is not satisfactory to assume a constant, externally given capital:output ratio, nor to adopt the doctrine that all new assets should have a low ratio. But there are far more important and fundamental points than this.

If for a moment we assume that a developing country is a closed system, then it is clear that its development process will have to take great heed of the need to produce all sorts of 'balances' in the flow of goods and services produced in future years. This is not just a matter of consumer preferences, where debate is legitimate about how far they should be allowed to dominate the character of output, in view of the varying difficulties in expanding particular types (and the varying *speeds* at which it can be done). It is even more important to secure a balance between the outputs (and hence supplies) of various *input* items (notably power, minerals, agricultural raw materials, etc), which are complementary to capital, so that the shortages of one can have a disproportionate effect on the output of final goods: and while this balance cannot be expected to be perfect in every year of the development process, we are *not* simply concerned with the position in the final year of (say) a five-year Plan, but also with the intervening years. Moreover, there is also the problem of providing adequately trained labour to work with the new types of capital equipment, as well as the necessary materials and transport facilities.

Fortunately international trade greatly reduces the difficulty of reconciling the types of goods and services which it is relatively easy to produce with the composition of those which a genuinely developing country wants to use for investment and consumption. This is particularly important for *machinery* (of which more will be wanted each year if growth is accelerated, and which is likely to present production problems, because there are so many different types) and for *essential raw materials*, which the country may be unable to produce on an adequate scale, for climatic reasons or through lack of mineral deposits.

Nevertheless, there are at least three powerful reasons why international trade, even in its widest sense, is not a cure-all for the problems of 'serious specific shortages':

(a) *Balance of payments.* The first is the all-too-familiar *balance-of-payments* problem. For reasons which vary from country to country, the scope for expanding exports usually has to be regarded as severely limited, especially in terms of the speed (measured in quinquennia) with which certain desired levels might be attained. Hence there is not an unlimited scope for 'covering' potential shortages of capital equipment, essential materials, spare parts etc. by means of imports. (I return to the balance-of-payments problems below.)

(b) *Essential local supplies.* Even where there is no balance-of-payments problem, for instance in certain oil countries, various key inputs cannot, effectively, be imported. *Electricity* is perhaps the most pervasive case: the physical things required for power generation and distribution may all be importable, but there are long *time-lags* between a decision to build and the flow of power to all users. Moreover, useable output does not automatically emerge as a continuous flow from the presence of the necessary capital equipment, even if the flow of fuel to the generators is reasonably assured: the system can all too easily have failures of one kind or another, which cause a break in the power supply to various users, often for a highly uncertain period. Such power failures are, of course, not unknown in developed countries, but only in exceptional cases (e.g. hospitals) do users consider it necessary to have their own emergency source of supply. In Nigeria, however, to take a case where the facts were made all too familiar to me, the unreliability of the public supply has driven most sizable users to spend very large sums in order to have their own emergency generators (including the residence of the World Bank's head).

In a similar way, *local transport* and *repair facilities* of many kinds have to be supplied internally, and deficiencies can hold back the growth of GDP quite seriously.

Usable *water* is a somewhat special case, which in some places is more important than anything else. The expensive process of *desalination* has provided an escape route for high-priority users in various countries, notably around the Gulf.

(c) *'Planning' development*. The development process is, as we have seen, a long-term affair, in which there are substantial time-lags between decisions to build new facilities and the emergence of the new output. Moreover, it is one in which new industries are commonly introduced, and the whole pattern of the economy slowly changes. Ideally, decisions about new projects should be related to *future* demands for the product in question, and allowances made for new facilities in the course of construction. If the various 'balances' discussed above are to be even roughly secured, decisions about new investment should be coordinated, since the future demand for (say) steel is much affected by the establishment of new engineering works (and the establishment of the new engineering works may also be greatly influenced, in a country with balance-of-payments problems, by the knowledge that new steel plants are being built). We are not likely to get good results from unrelated investment decisions by entrepreneurs who are much influenced by the current position and moved by varying amounts of 'animal spirits'.

The whole planning process is much too big a subject to tackle here, and is a terribly difficult one when there are so many unknowns (including the scale of future aid and the conditions which donors or foreign investors may impose on the projects for which it is used). I set out my early views in *The Development of the Indian Economy* (1962), and the appendices on *time-lags* and *phasing* are particularly relevant. In the main I have no reason to change these views. I still find it useful to emphasise the crucial distinction between the value of projects *started* in a plan period, the *expenditure* in the period (whether on old projects or new ones, including in both cases projects not likely to be finished by the end of the period), and the value of the projects *completed* in the period (which is what influences the rise in output of the product concerned). In recent years, however, I have found myself much concerned with a special aspect of this: how should a government allocate the limited expenditure which it can do each year, when it has started so many projects in the past that it cannot provide funds to carry on with all of them at the technically optimum speed? (I return to that topic below.)

This last type of work reflects a constructive attempt to advise governments which have got into a mess on what they should do in order to get out of it, rather than simply saying, 'if you want to have a good system for managing your capital expenditure, you should not start from here'. There is, however, still a case for indicating the sort of system which it would be good to establish in the long run. On this I can only set out a few *obiter dicta*:

(a) I join with many others in supporting the target of a rolling five-year plan (or three-year, or four-year, according to country), which will be partly indicative (especially on private-sector activities) and partly operational – though later-year figures will be reconsidered each year in the light of the lastest information, when the plan is rolled forward. This plan should be coupled with an annual development programme, which is an operational document showing what government expenditure is allocated to each project (or group of smaller projects) in the coming year.

(b) The crucial thing about the five-year plan is that it should be *realistic*, and not reflect wild hopes about aid, or about output increases which would only be realised if everything went rather better than a responsible person's most optimistic estimate.

(c) Ideally, the expenditure on major projects should be, at least provisionally, phased between the years, and some projects would be clearly shown as *not* due to be completed within the period (and not *starting* in the early years). This may, however, be too difficult a rule to enforce, especially as donors would not yet have been found for some projects. One may have to be content with a *negative* rule, that projects for which a firm starting date is not shown are only provisionally in the plan at all: a special mark should be attached to those which will only be started if a satisfactory external donor can be found.

(d) Formally, the plan should cover privately financed capital expenditure, as well as the public sector, so as to get an overall picture. To some extent (depending on the control system, if any, which is considered desirable) private expenditure on key projects can be regulated by the government, or done according to an agreed scheme. To an increasing extent, however, I have come to doubt the wisdom of making almost all capital expenditure subject to a licence, and issuing these only for projects which fall within the plan: government planners cannot be expected to have enough knowledge to prepare fully detailed plans, or the bureaucratic skill to operate a looser system on a more discretionary basis through local offices. Delays in securing approval can have serious consequences.

4. BALANCE-OF-PAYMENTS PROBLEMS

To some extent balance-of-payments problems have inevitably appeared in the above discussion, because they are so crucial to the development of most LDCs: for that very reason, however, it is useful to bring the various aspects together in a single section.

First, there is the traditional point that there may be two distinct reasons why a developing country suffers such problems. If one considers only *aggregative* analysis, there is the 'savings gap': the country tries to do an amount of internal investment which exceeds the domestic saving (including *government* saving) which it is prepared to do, even when working to capacity, by more than it can obtain as aid or sustainable capital inflow. The result is a loss of exchange reserves, or the piling up of commercial debts (i.e. 'arrears' of payments under a system of exchange control).

Possible remedies for the savings gap include a cut in investment expenditure, which will probably slow up development, or a successful savings campaign – including measures to raise *government saving*, e.g. by more effective tax collection – or an increase in aid (or other capital inflows).

On the other hand, if one recognises the likelihood of numerous *specific* shortages or potential shortages, one may meet a balance-of-payments gap, this is because operation of the economy at anything like full capacity would require a supply of materials, spares, essential consumer goods and capital goods, etc. which exceeds the domestic output of these things by more than the achievable export proceeds, plus aid and other net capital inflows. Internal demand may be high enough to secure full-capacity output, if the balance-of-payments deficit can be covered by running down exchange reserves, etc., but it is likely that activity will be kept below potential, largely through the inadequacy of inputs.

If we consider the remedies which were mentioned above for the savings gap, we can say that more aid would cover the balance-of-payment gap (and also provide more funds for investment, to replace those precariously derived from selling exchange reserves); on the other hand a cut in investment, or a successful savings campaign, will largely serve to lower activity further, though a by-product of this will be the reduction (or even ending) of the reserve loss.

There is, however, a further possibility. If the developed countries can be persuaded to increase the trade opportunities open to the developing country in their market, by being willing to buy more of things which it can easily produce (e.g. textiles) then this will reduce, or even eliminate, the balance-of-payments gap. It may be necessary to complement the expansion of exports with (say) extra taxes to raise total savings, plus aid, to the level of investment, and avoid the creation of a savings gap. The slogan 'trade, not aid' is usually an excellent one, but it requires the corollary that if aid is in fact cancelled in the process an increased savings effort is needed to maintain the old level of investment.

It may well be asked whether there are any other ways of closing (or narrowing) the balance-of-payments gap, without reducing the level of internal activity. One answer is that *exchange controls* (of which import controls are a sub-species) are frequently introduced with the object of reducing non-essential imports and other foreign payments, 'so as to concentrate the available external purchasing power on essentials'. On the export side there may also be various schemes for (in effect) subsidising exports, or 'non-traditional exports', by giving them concessions under the exchange control system. The trouble is that the balance-of-payments gap still seems to persist in so many cases; I consider some of the problems of 'controls' in Section 5.

The classic answer, beloved by the IMF, is that inflationary finance should be eliminated (which they hope will have no more than a temporary effect on activity) and that competitive power should be improved, largely by setting a 'realistic' exchange rate. This would serve to stimulate exports and restrain imports, with both factors tending to raise the level of local production.

On this I usually find myself agreeing that the exchange rate is too high, and wanting to help forward export production and import substitution by having a more realistic one. But the problem seldom seems to me capable of a full solution by these methods alone, even in conjunction with exchange control. In Bangladesh, for example, where export proceeds (including emigrants' remittances – a most important item) commonly cover only about one-half of the imports regarded by the aid consortium as 'essential', I find it virtually impossible to envisage what commodities could *both* be produced on the necessary scale *and* command an export market, or replace imports, in such a way as to do much to reduce the gap: indeed, the problem is in danger of worsening, through the growth of population and the doubtful future of jute and jute goods (the major exports). Even the opening up of markets for textiles, etc. in developed countries seems likely to do relatively little, if the same opportunities are open to other developing countries as well.

There is clearly something in common with this problem and the difficulties which Keynes analysed over the payment of German reparations. One needs to be very careful, however, about exactly what question or questions one is trying to answer. If one is wanting to decide whether it is wise to adopt some policy, for example devaluation, one is primarily concerned to assess how much better or worse the position in future years would be *with* the policy rather than *without* it: there may be difficulties about deciding what 'consequential actions' would be taken with the policy, as a result of introducing it, but essentially one is comparing two alternative possibilities for future years.[6] One is not trying to assess what that future will be like, or how it will compare with the present.

For deciding on the long-term viability or progress of a developing country, however, one must necessarily consider all the factors which will affect it. Essentially one is concerned with *long-term* developments, and all sorts of things may change, sometimes in ways that can be roughly predicted. Even if one is interested (for the moment) only in the future balance-of-payments position, one cannot ignore things like the growth of population or the progress of plastics in replacing jute: it is useless to confine oneself to an assessment of the 'effects' of devaluation, or some other policy. A 'scenario' approach for *development through time* is needed – and obviously a whole family of scenarios may be better, using different assumptions about various exogenous factors. 'Short-cut' and 'semi-intuitional' approaches may be useful, but they must be directed at the right problem.

A few special points may be useful in this field, particularly for people who have not had the privilege of learning by experience how dangerous some apparently plausible assumptions may be – particularly those embodied in 'small country' models, under which it is assumed that the country in question can sell as much as it chooses to put on the world market at an externally determined world price.

In the first place, of course, the country in question is often not 'small' in relation to the world market for the most relevant products: jute and jute manufacturers from Bangladesh are a clear-cut example, and these account for well over half of Bangladesh exports. With jute manufactures in particular the products are heterogeneous and sold on markets which are far from perfect, so that both 'price' and 'marketing devices' are matters on which decisions have to be made; and these are influenced by the actions, or expected reactions, of rival producers.

Next, for simple manufactures (e.g. clothing) a country may be a small enough producer for its actions to have a negligible effect on the behaviour of rival producers, but the market may be of such a fragmented kind (with orders depending, for instance, on 'connections') that the country's exporters certainly cannot sell whatever quantity they choose to offer – even if they are prepared to make price cuts which are much bigger than the price 'shading', which might perhaps be regarded as consistent with the theory.

Next, there is the awful warning from Nigerian oil. Nigeria is not a big producer in relation to world output (under 2 per cent), or even OPEC output (about 5 per cent), but its production is restrained by OPEC decisions – not decisively, but effectively enough for the quantity exported to have been forced down to about one-half of the 1980 level. Since oil represents about 95 per cent of Nigerian exports, it is clear that devaluation (which I strongly support, since the present rate is totally unrealistic) will not have much scope for increasing exports, except perhaps in the very long run. And assessments of the future balance-of-payments position cannot possibly rest on the over-simplified assumption that Nigeria can export as much oil as it likes at a price which is exogenously determined (even though the price *is* more or less exogenously determined).

Finally, there is a point which is perhaps of more relevance to the IMF than to a single country. Suppose that policies of devaluation and restriction of internal demand were recommended only to one developing country, which was equipped to produce a fair range of exportable primary products on a modest, but increasable, scale, and that these products were sold on a world market which was reasonably 'perfect'. The reactions of rival producers might be negligible and the effect on that country's balance of payments might well be excellent. But if the same policy is prescribed for a whole series of broadly similiar developing countries, the combined effect on the world markets may be big falls in price, perhaps followed by the organisation of restriction schemes: the balance-of-payments problems may be solved by the effect of deflation on imports, to the chagrin of exporters in developed countries, but the contribution from increased exports of primary products may be negative.

5. EXCHANGE CONTROLS

As noted above, it is common for developing countries with persistent balance-of-payments problems to introduce some sort of exchange controls, with the object of trying to bring some national judgement to bear on how the limited flow of foreign exchange shall be used. This raises a whole host of problems, and I can do no more than advance a few *obiter dicta* about some of them.

First, it seems to me clearly wrong to assume, in a world of imperfect markets, that the problem can always be solved by the choice of a sufficiently low exchange rate. For safety I might add some qualifying clause, such as 'without creating other problems which are worse than the disease', but this would only be to emphasise that we have to be concerned with *practicable* measures. The *time factor* is, however, important: a low rate might, if no disturbances occurred, produce a solution in five years.

Secondly, it is nevertheless true that developing countries frequently seek to maintain exchange rates which are so high that the working of the controls is made much more difficult, and the remedial processes which might ease the position are hampered. Without trying to define the ideal rate for an essentially disequilibrium position, I am in favour of one which *helps* to facilitate controls and supplements whatever other measures (or 'natural forces') are working for improvement.

Thirdly, the controls must be virtually comprehensive, subject to *de minimis* clauses or to deliberate exclusions made to further some praiseworthy objective. In particular, controls should not be confined to imports of goods: services and export of capital should be covered as well, since they use up the available foreign exchange.

Fourthly, it is nevertheless usually wise to have a direct control on imports (i.e. the physical landing of goods), as well as a control on the purchase of foreign exchange to pay for them. This is desirable in the interests of enforcement of the exchange controls. It is notoriously difficult to prevent the citizens of a country from acquiring the means to pay for imports illegally, for example by failing to surrender the whole of their receipts of foreign exchange from exports, visible or invisible, as required by the regulations, or by using 'off-set' transactions, or by over-invoicing legal imports. If there is no control on physical imports, luxury goods can be brought in and sold at enormous profit, because no foreign exchange is issued to buy them legally. A would-be importer who obtains an import licence should receive an exchange permit 'automatically'.

Fifthly, the control process needs to start with a 'foreign exchange review' for the following year, or possible half-year. This includes estimates of incomings (including aid and capital items) and a tentative set of figures for each kind of outgoings (again including capital items). International discussion of these figures may help to produce more incomings (e.g. loans or aid) or postponement of outgoings (e.g. through rescheduling agreements). But in the end the 'review' has to lead to a plan of action, or foreign exchange budget, which the government can expect to be able to enforce through its controls. (A 'contingency' item, and allowances for evasion, may be thought wise.)

The implementation of the 'plan of action', or 'foreign exchange budget' raises a whole host of technical problems, over and above the 'decision' problems about objectives (e.g. 'development' versus 'materials to foster employment', usually in consumer goods industries; or the allocation between types of consumer goods).

These technical problems are extremely complicated (and also extremely important) and only a few of them can be sketched here. They arise largely out of the need to allocate the licences between individual firms, which may be *merchants* who would re-sell the goods, or *industrial users*, who import materials and spares for use in their own business. If only the first existed, it would seem natural for the planners to decide how much foreign exchange should be spent on each commodity group which they wished to treat separately, and to issue licences to importing firms in proportion to their past trade in that commodity group. But for industrial users it is vital that they should receive a reasonably balanced supply of the different input items, since otherwise they may be able to produce very little for lack of some essential ingredients or spare parts. It seems best, therefore, to arrange for each industrial user to have a single licence covering all his requirements (or perhaps two or three, each covering broad types), and to leave it to him to make a sensible selection. He may well use it for inputs in quite different proportions from his past usage, because the scope for using local substitutes may vary between items, and it may be possible to vary the products to save on particular imports (e.g. expensive dyes).

There will be statistical problems arising out of combining a *commodity approach*, based on import statistics, for goods imported by merchants, with a *user approach* for things bought by industrial users, especially as some goods will come under both categories: but I cannot deal with these here.

The really difficult problems arise out of the division of the import licences (or exchange permits for invisibles) between individual firms. A licence is, of course, a very valuable thing, even if, say, a user buys materials for his own business. The obtaining from each firm of reliable figures for past imports coming within each separate commodity group is far from easy, and the assessment of the imported materials needed by an industrial user to run his factory at x per cent of capacity, with a variety of products, may be yet harder, even if there is agreement on the value of x for products of that degree of 'essentiality'. The whole operation of licence issue is so formidable that a 'systematic' issue can usually be made only once every half-year – though there will have to be some sort of provision for discretionary special issues to individual applicants at other times, for example for capital goods to replace those worn out, or for various invisibles, or for 'emergencies'.

In a way a six-monthly issue fits in with the planning of purchases by many firms, especially where goods are not bought from stock. But it also raises *timing* problems, to reconcile a foreign exchange budget for licence issues in, say, January with goods largely arriving in the second half of the year (but with a large variation) and payments at varying intervals after that. The natural basis for the budget is 'expected receipts of foreign exchange in the coming half-year', and one needs a substantial exchange reserve to deal with lags and their variations.

There is an obvious case for doing something to appropriate to the government a major part of the 'rent' which accrues to the recipient of a licence, whatever use he makes of it. Not only is this *equitable*, it also makes the controls *easier to operate*, because it reduces the pressure of applicants to obtain these licences by means of plausible stories, support from influential friends, and straight corruption.

Probably the most fruitful approach is to have a charge for an import licence which varies between commodity groups and between categories of industrial user, according to the 'essentiality' of the final product(s). The authorities will still decide on the foreign exchange to be used for each commodity group, or type of user, so that they know what to allow in their foreign exchange budget; and of course they can still control the allocation of the scarce foreign exchange according to a national assessment of priorities, instead of allowing rich buyers of luxury items to outbid industrial users, who would 'give employment', perhaps to produce necessities for the poor.

There is, of course, nothing in this to prevent *open general licences* for specified goods and services if this is considered desirable in the existing exchange position. The foreign exchange budget then requires an *estimate* of the amount which will be spent under these licences, and errors in this may be very large if traders suspect that they may be reversed at a later date. But the economic and administrative gains can be substantial, particularly with materials and spare parts.

It is sometimes suggested that the complications of issuing licences and exchange permits could be avoided altogether by having (so long as the shortage of foreign exchange remains) high tariffs, which can vary between goods in a way that reflects 'social priorities'. There are, however, difficulties about this, even if the complications of GATT and most-favoured-nation clauses can be ignored:

a) Tariffs do nothing to prevent the export of capital, which could absorb all available foreign exchange: something is needed to deal with this, and it is hard to achieve without a comprehensive system of exchange control
b) Estimates of imports will have to be made for the foreign exchange budget, and these may prove very faulty (especially if traders suspect a reversion to controls).

(c) It is difficult to apply tariffs to *services*, so that there may have to be exchange controls (with charges) for these.

A half-way house is sometimes suggested, whereby the price mechanism, in the form of auction or tenders, would be used to distribute import licences, rather than an allocation system. The authorities would decide, in the light of the foreign exchange budget, how much foreign exchange would be released for each commodity group, and auction the licences. This idea has uses on pure consumer goods, but raises serious difficulties for industrial users: makers of luxuries and makers of poor men's wares may use the same materials or intermediates, and the latter may be squeezed out; and individual factories may get highly ill-balanced assortments of inputs, particularly if tenders are used.

Finally, there is the problem of exports. I have assumed in the above that a 'reasonable' exchange rate is fixed; but even so production for export will be unattractive as compared with production for the starved home market, unless some special measure is adopted. The easiest way is to have a system of 'rewarding' exporters with a free import licence for a vaguely equivalent amount of imported inputs, which would be transferable: this would be over and above the licences which the factory got in the general way, on the basis of capacity and 'essentiality' of product or products.

Alternatively, a cash subsidy may be used, and/or specially generous rewards may be given for non-traditional exports: the reward can, of course, be varied according to the product or product-group. The one disastrous policy, all too often adopted, is to have a ridiculously over-valued currency and no special help for exporters except perhaps in a few cases.

Phasing-out of Controls

One last point is that *if* the country's external position improves, perhaps through more generous aid, then these various schemes can easily be phased out, for example by lowering the charge for import licences, or by making more foreign exchange available, or by extending the open general licence scheme to more products. *Pace* the IMF, however, I do not think it sensible to assume that this is something which *will* happen: 'and so they lived happily ever after', with no controls and a good speed of development, is not a particularly common occurrence in developing countries.

6. MANAGEMENT OF A CAPITAL EXPENDITURE PROGRAMME

Section 3 dealt briefly with the shape which a well-run capital expenditure programme should take, and its relation to a five-year plan and an annual development plan. This section explains briefly why programmes so often seem to get into a chaotic state, and the sort of method which I have recommended in Bangladesh and Nigeria for getting back on course.

The best starting point is the fact that capital expenditure is not just a single, undifferentiated flow of money, but covers a multitude of very different projects, with very different gestation periods. Moreover the Government never starts with a virgin sheet: at all times there are bound to be projects at every stage in the process of planning and execution, from initial conception of the broad idea, through feasibility studies, site selection, preparation of detailed specifications, tendering, start of the work, and, finally, completion. Different types of expenditure are commonly in the hands of different ministries or other agencies, each with a likely interest in its own projects. External donors of funds for particular projects are similarly interested primarily in these.

For understandable reasons, five-year plans are liable to be optimistic documents, which tend to exaggerate the total amount of funds likely to be available, and to understate the probable cost of projects and the time needed to complete them. There is pressure to get a lot of projects included in the plan, often with no proper phasing of the expenditure. The cost of completing, or simply continuing, projects already begun is often understated, and little allowance is made for emergency expenditures (caused, for example, by a cyclone) which may be needed.

The result is all too commonly that far too many projects get *started*, if only in a rather nominal way; the producers of the annual development plan are liable to find that the funds which are actually (or even *probably*) available for the coming year are not sufficient to cover the expenditures which it would be desirable to spend on the ongoing projects, if they are to progress at the technically desirable pace. 'The tyranny of on-going projects means that I can never start on high-priority new ones' was the depressing, if slightly exaggerated, summary of the position given to me by the Deputy Chairman of the Bangladesh Planning Commission in 1974.

Further reasons for this situation emerging are the small amounts of cash needed per year for the early stages of a project, the difficulty of resisting external assistance offered by donors (even though local currency will have to be provided by the government for local expenditure), the difficulty of closing many types of project when 'extensions' seem attractive, and – particularly in the case of Nigeria – a big fall in the available flow of funds, caused by a fall in oil revenue.

The natural reaction to this sort of situation is to spread the available funds thinly over all the on-going projects. In Bangladesh the annual allocations to the various ministries and agencies in the first two years of the second five-year plan followed almost exactly the proportions which had been shown by the plan document, even though the amounts were far lower than the plan showed: 'priority for agriculture', which was supposedly the basis of the plan, did not apply when it would have required the acceptance by other ministries of differentiated cuts from the proportions which had been so painfully agreed. The trouble with this is, of course, that very few projects get completed, and in general it is only the *completion* of a project which produces any extra output.

The proposed solution for Bangladesh was to make a realistic

ssessment of the funds which it seemed reasonably *certain* would
be available in each of the last three years of the plan period.
About 80 per cent of these amounts were to be guaranteed to the
various Ministries, but not in the Second Five Year Plan propor-
ions: the actual proportions would be decided after a debate on
priorities, for which a few ground rules were suggested.
Moreover, a condition of this guaranteed allocation was to be the
election by each ministry of a limited number of 'core' projects,
which would in total require about that amount of funding if
carried out at a 'proper' speed: both the selection (and the time-
able for the completion of this limited number of projects) was
o be agreed with the planning commission, which would be able
o monitor performance on these core projects fairly effectively.
n this way arrangements would be made to ensure that at least
he core part of the plan would (almost certainly) be properly
executed, and 'deliver its fruits in due season'.

   The proposal added that at the start of each year a careful up-
o-date estimate would be made of the total funds likely to be
available, in the same way as in the past. If, as was probable, this
exceeded the sum of the guaranteed allocations, the allocation of
he surplus should be decided by the usual bargaining process.
As a fall-back, but *not* an optimum solution, the principle might
be to calculate the total allocation which each Ministry would
have received under the SFYP proportions. For 'priority' Minis-
ries this might well be less than their guaranteed allocation, and
hey would simply receive the guaranteed amount: the surplus
would be distributed between the other Ministries in proportion
o the excess of their SFYP figure over their guaranteed alloca-
ion. Ministries were to be largely left to their own devices over
he use of these uncertain, and rather small, funds.

   An illustrative table showed how this 'fall-back' system would
probably give the priority Ministries a rather high proportion of
he total funds for the year, especially if the funds which actually
became available did not exceed the amount initially regarded as
reasonably certain. The really important benefit of the system
was, however, that a selected set of core projects would be
executed at a proper speed; this would remain true however the

guaranteed funds were distributed. Some guidance was provided about the selection of core projects, the most important point being that the prospective benefits from getting the project completed were to be set against the expenditure which still had to be incurred, ignoring money already spent.[7]

In Nigeria the drastic fall in oil revenues had produced a similar problem of a hopelessly overloaded investment programme, but the institutional arrangements were different. The case for a 'core' approach was again accepted when put forward by the World Bank Mission (in which I handled this part of the work), with the slight elaboration that all projects above a minimum size should be put in one of four categories:

(a) Core projects, to be completed at the speed which is desirable on technical grounds. (These must not absorb more funds than will certainly be available.)
(b) Projects to be abandoned, from which any assets usuable elsewhere (e.g. land) would be sold or diverted to other projects.
(c) Projects on which work would continue, but only at a pace made possible by the funds which remained in each year after a full allocation to the core projects.
(d) Projects which would be moth-balled, in the hope that they would be restarted at some future date, and executed at a proper pace. (The slow and uncertain progress likely to be achieved in category (c) seemed too costly.)

In view of the great over-load, *new* projects would have to be excluded for the time being. There would, however, have to be an annual review, at which a new core list would be prepared. All the projects on the previous list would reappear, unless they had been completed (or unless a drastic change in circumstances led to one or more being dropped): the essence of the core idea is to get some projects *completed*. In addition, projects on the non-core list (and possibly some new projects) might be added to the core list, provided the assured funds could justify this: such promotion of non-core projects to core status is preferable to raising slightly the speed of execution of all non-core projects.

This proposal (and more detailed proposals about the quarterly releases of funds to Ministries) was to be accompanied by the introduction of a rolling three-year capital budget, for which a procedure was outlined: the provisional figures for three years ahead which each Ministry received would give it a better basis on which to plan ahead. The whole package was welcomed by the Nigerians, who proceeded to try to implement much of it more rapidly than its cautious originator had thought it wise to suggest.

7. SOME CONCLUDING REMARKS

It would be nice to end this paper with a neat summing-up about the relevance of Keynesian ideas in developing countries, but that is really beyond my powers. What I have learned in my work on developing countries is that one has to be particularly careful to think what *other* considerations have *also* to be taken into account when forming a judgement on any practical problem. This is of course also true when one is working in a *developed* country, but the implicit assumptions on which one works have to be somewhat different – and when working in one's own country one does not always realise what one is assuming, because it has become a part of one's whole thinking.[8]

It may perhaps be useful to destroy one popular reason for thinking that Keynesian ideas are inapplicable in underdeveloped countries, which simply equates these with a simple-minded caricature of those ideas. A countervailing caricature of the argument might run as follows:

Diagnosis allegedly based on Keynesian ideas: Underdeveloped countries suffer from unemployment and low real income per head because they have inadequate capital. The remedy for both problems is to increase investment. In the short run, the extra demand will reduce unemployment, and somewhat raise the real national income; in the long run, the use of the successive inflows of extra capital will raise real income per worker progressively. There is no need to worry about how to finance the extra investment: investment creates its own saving.

The critic then produces a whole host of reasons for not accepting such a simple-minded analysis. For example:

(a) In the short-run, it may be difficult to carry out the investment projects, for lack of facilities in the industries making and installing capital goods: at the very least, the investment schemes will normally have a very high import content.

(b) Even if the investment schemes are confined to rural roads and the like, made by primitive methods with baskets, etc. which are available, the extra demand which is supposed to produce multiplier effects will be largely directed to things which are either not produced internally at all, or for which there are no spare production facilities (even though labour is available). Food is an important component, in which output is not dependent on orders, and often cannot be increased.

(c) Even if imports can be increased (e.g. under an expanded aid programme) there are likely to be bottlenecks on essential local supplies, notably power or repair facilities.

   My reply to this is not that the critic's analysis is incorrect, but simply that he is tilting at a man of straw. Even in developed countries the allegedly Keynesian analysis would be oversimplified, especially if the economy is a very open one: in developing countries the danger of inadequate local facilities is greater, but the need to consider *all* the consequences of increasing investment is not confined to them.[9] Keynesian ideas are much wider than the above caricature would suggest, as explained in Section 1.

There may of course be occasions when an underdeveloped country would benefit from Keynesian measures to increase internal demand: in some years I have felt that this was true of India, but never studied the matter in depth. If so, then such measures should be introduced.

In the main, however, the problem in developing countries is to secure a progressive, long-term rise in their output potential per head, in the face of the various obstacles of initial low starting-point, the poverty trap, population growth, inadequacy of local facilities of many kinds, the balance-of-payments problem, etc. On some aspects of this Keynesian ideas are clearly very relevant, for example 'How to Pay for the War', the balance-of-payments problem, international organisations (e.g. the World Bank). This is not, however, to claim that they constitute a unique basis for analysing problems, since many others have worked on the subject. Moreover, it is nearly always necessary to draw on more than one source of ideas: my own experience is that the supplementary sources are most frequently common sense, flexibility of ideas and a recognition that administrative procedures must be workable by the sort of people who will have to operate them.

In the more narrowly economic field, I found myself rather ill-prepared in three respects, though this is probably a reflection on me rather than on the economic literature in general or on Keynes in particular. These were:

(a) I did not instinctively work on a sufficiently disaggregated basis, or appreciate the potentially crucial importance of specific input shortages.

(b) I was not well adjusted to thinking of time sequences, notably the distinctive roles of project starts, capital expenditure in a year and project completions.[1] The literature on growth theory which I had read seemed to deal exclusively with a single concept, which was both investment in the period and the addition to capital in use.

(c) My economic reading had not led me to appreciate the complexities and limitations of 'the capital:output ratio', which in fact varies enormously between different types of capital asset, and which should have a different magnitude for answering different questions, even in macroeconomic terms. Nor had it led me to realise that one of the main objects in policy making is to find ways in which output can be raised without additional capital, or the capital:output ratio lowered.[11]

NOTES

1. Moreover, one must not forget the schemes which were not in the event adopted as part of the Bretton Woods outcome, such as the establishment of buffer stocks, or of a commodity-related international currency.
2. I find it useful to compare the Government's problem with that of the investment committee for my College's portfolio. We know that we do not have even 1 per cent of the information ideally needed to assist us in our proclaimed objective of having a policy which can be expected to produce reasonable results in real terms over the next century or two. But we know we have to make decisions, although we also know that we have made plenty of mistakes; and we are reasonably satisfied with the results of the first thirty-two years. (Those interested in this illustration of the problem created by uncertainty will find an account in the paper which I gave to the AUTE in 1979, which appeared in *Macroeconomic Analysis*, edited by Currie, Nobay and Peel, published by Croom Helm.)
3. This point was brought home to me vividly on going to a job in Argentina in 1963. There seemed no justification for classing it as an underdeveloped country (there had been an underground railway in Buenos Aires before the First World War!). 'Mismanaged' seemed to be an adjective which threw more light on its problems and opportunities.
4. Some of these points are getting to the border between aggregate and disaggregated analysis, and are elaborated below.
5. One is reminded of the young boy who found that his job of opening and shutting the furnace door could be 'delegated' to a piece of string attached to a part of the machinery. The saving of labour (not, in this case, the increase of output) is better attributed to the *idea* rather than to the capital embodied in the string. (See also the discussion of the capital:output ratio below.)
6. This is analogous to the question which I discussed in my book *The Effects of UK Direct Investment Overseas* (Cambridge University Press, 1967), except that in that book the comparison was between the present and what the position might have been: but again this is a comparison between two alternatives for the same date(s). (See in particular Chapter 2.)
7. I was unable to discuss this proposal with the people concerned, because the document was not completed until the last morning of my visit (the whole proposal being a by-product of the job for which I had really been invited – a common feature of my work in developing countries). But on a later visit to a different Ministry I gathered that the 'core' system was not operating, and the World Bank officers had almost ceased to grumble about the ADP system.
8. I have discussed this in my article 'The Economics of Under-developed Countries' (*Economic Journal*, March 1963).
9. See, for example, my Keynes lecture to the British Academy, published by that body in its proceedings for 1983, and also in a separate pre-print.
10. As usual, once one gets the answer it seems obvious. I cleaned up my own ideas in an article on time-lags, which is reproduced as Appendix A in my book on India (*The Development of The Indian Economy*, London: George Allen

& Unwin, 1962). An English non-economist's comment was, 'Well, that is all very clear, but it seems so obvious that I do not see why you need to write it'; but many officials concerned with Indian planning said that it would remove much confusion from the work on the third plan.

11. See Section 3 above, and Appendix C of my book on the Indian economy.

DISCUSSION

Official Discussant, Hans Singer: I find comment difficult for each of these two papers, although for different reasons. In the case of Professor Thirlwall's paper, the main reason is that I find so little with which to disagree; the reader can confirm this by looking at my own contribution in this volume. In the case of Brian Reddaway's paper my difficulty is that it deals more with investment allocation and planning problems than with the broad macroeconomic sweep. This is a very important contribution in adding the 'nitty gritty' to Keynesian macroeconomics; Keynes as a practical man would I think have thoroughly approved of this paper. However, as Brian Reddaway himself acknowledges, it is not easy to apply the labels of 'Keynesian' or 'non-Keynesian' when you come down to this more detailed and practical level of analysis at which it is more a matter of judgement and common sense than of macroeconomic views.

All the same, Brian Reddaway, like Tony Thirlwall, has no hesitation in answering the question of Keynes' interest in problems of development and of his relevance to developing countries today in the affirmative. Both point out that quite apart from the 'domestic' Keynes there was also the 'international' Keynes of Bretton Woods – Keynes I and Keynes II as I call them – and there can be no possible doubt about the relevance of the international Keynes. But even the domestic Keynes is felt and shown by both authors to have something to teach us in development economics.

Both papers also refer to Keynes' interest in commodity price stabilisation, international buffer stocks and commodity-related international currency. The relevance of this after a long period of falling commodity prices, and the role of the upheaval in the oil market in the collapse of the Bretton Woods system, can leave no doubt about the importance of the views and proposals put forward in this field by Keynes, but alas, not implemented. To begin with a minor quibble, the Thirlwall paper is perhaps underplaying Keynes' interest in this problem by saying that he became preoccupied with commodity problems 'towards the end of his life' (p. 12). In fact, as indeed Professor Thirlwall himself points out later in his paper, Keynes' 'preoccupation' is already clearly expressed in his 1938 paper to the British Association and at least coincides with, but probably precedes, the *General Theory*. I think it was a tragedy for the Bretton Woods system that not only were Keynes' more far-reaching proposals on commodities disregarded, but also that the 'third leg' of the Bretton Woods system, the International Trade Organisation (ITO), was never established. As a speculation, I would venture the guess that if Keynes had realised that the ITO was not going to be established he might have wished to withdraw his support from the incomplete Bretton Woods system which emerged. GATT, which took the place of the ITO, contained none of the things which Keynes thought important, and stood for some things which Keynes in fact fought against.

Professor Thirlwall in his paper refers to Joan Robinson and quotes disguised unemployment as one of the contributions of Keynesianism to development economics. I should have thought that Joan Robinson's imperfect competition would have at least an equal claim to be quoted. With international trade, and specifically also trade in primary commodities, dominated by monopolistic and oligopolistic production and trading structures, it is to the theory of imperfect competition rather than to the analysis of Marshallian elasticities that we must look for understanding and policy guidance.

Yet another minor quibble with Professor Thirlwall is where he quotes Harrod, Joan Robinson and Kaldor as those to whom Keynes gave the tools to provide a framework for the analysis of long-run growth in developing countries. I feel that Colin Clark should be specifically added to this group and not be submerged in the anonymity of 'and others'. The national income framework of analysis developed first by Clark on the basis of the

Keynesian concepts, and then further developed by Stone and Seers, is surely the most striking preservation of the Keynesian heritage in current development planning and development discussion.

Both papers emphasise that in the Keynesian system of using finance for turning the stone of unemployment and idle resources into the bread of economic development there is a special role for the state as the source of ultimate finance and also to provide the essential infrastructure and complementarity in investment which the Reddaway paper emphasises, but also for entre-preneurial initiative and 'animal spirits'.

The Reddaway paper makes an interesting point (p. 36) in drawing attention to the fact that in 'How to Pay for the War' Keynes was concerned with a situation where demand had to be constrained rather than increased and that this situation is close to the problems of many developing countries. It would be an interesting exercise to go through 'How to Pay for the War', replace 'the War' by 'development expenditures', as Brian Reddaway suggests, and then see to what extent it can serve as a treatise on financing development. The organisation of the British war economy in the Second World War under Keynes' guidance could be a model for developing (as well as developed) countries in yet another even more vital respect. How to achieve the natural rate of increase, i.e. how to organise for full produc-tion, full employment, full utilisation of all available resources and yet at the same time restructure incomes and entitlement in such a way that in spite of rationing and restraints on demand, economic welfare is promoted rather than reduced. In that sense I would say the most direct relevance of Keynes for developing countries today is as a guide towards 'development with a human face', to borrow a term which Richard Jolly uses in a different context.[1]

(Owing to a shortage of time, there was no discussion from the floor – Editor.)

NOTE

1. The reference is to his Barbara Ward lecture on 'Adjustment with a human
    face' at the SID (Society for International Development) World Conference
    in Rome, 1985.

WHAT KEYNES AND KEYNESIANISM CAN TEACH US ABOUT LESS DEVELOPED COUNTRIES
Hans Singer

It would be possible to make out a convincing case arguing that Keynes' teaching is highly relevant and important for less developed countries (LDCs), both for their domestic policies and for their international relations in the kind of world system which Keynes was so influential in helping to create at Bretton Woods. But it has also been argued that Keynes is not relevant – or is even misleading – in the circumstances of LDCs, or that the international system he helped to create is irrelevant or harmful to them. This apparent conflict of views is partly a tribute to the wide range of Keynes' contribution, with those declaring Keynes relevant and their opponents selecting different elements of his contribution. To another extent it represents conflicts of views among those concerned with LDCs. Some development economists are 'Keynesian', others are anti-Keynesians. The split between the Keynesians and anti-Keynesians applies to development economists as well as those concerned with other aspects of economics.

The view held by this author and expressed in this contribution is that certainly some aspects of Keynes' teaching are highly relevant to LDCs; that these relevant aspects are often related to Keynes' overall philosophy and methodology rather than to the details of his prescriptions; that the relevance of Keynes is particularly strong in the international field (the Keynes of Bretton Woods, or Keynes II as I shall call him) as distinct from the domestic Keynes of the *General Theory*[1] (Keynes I); that the importance of Keynes, in the international field in particular, lies often in those parts of his thinking and recommendations which were not implemented rather than in those which were; that even in those aspects in which his teaching may not be directly applicable to the conditions of LDCs the careful study of his views can still lead us to useful policy suggestions for those in charge of the destinies of the LDCs to ponder.

On the relevance of Keynes' overall philosophy and methodology our best starting point is the well-known essay by Albert Hirschman[2] on 'The Rise and Decline of Development Economics'. Hirschman credits Keynes specifically with two major methodological breakthroughs which in his view make Keynes not only relevant for development thinking but in fact the founder of mainstream development economics. The two breakthroughs singled out by Hirschman are as follows:

(a) On the domestic side Keynes in the *General Theory* moved away from the classical (and neo-classical) vision of mono-economics, i.e. the view that the laws of economics and precepts of economic policy are universal and apply everywhere and in all circumstances. Instead, the *General Theory* is based on a picture of duo-economics, i.e. that there is one set of economic relations and policies applicable to conditions of unemployment of resources, and another to conditions of full employment. This could then easily be extended to distinguishing the economics applying to fully developed countries from those in a state of underdevelopment.

(b) On the international side, Keynes – the Bretton Woods Keynes – through his vision of a new order of post-war international economic relations developed a framework and a precept of policies by which the developing countries could be brought into a network of international relations to the mutual benefit of both themselves and the industrial countries.

DOMESTIC RELEVANCE

The 'domestic' shift from classical monoeconomics towards

Keynesian duo-economics was important to development thinking in three different ways:

(a) Most generally, Keynes' idea that it was possible, indeed necessary, by macroeconomic policies and where necessary intervention, to stimulate economic potential which the market mechanism allows to go to waste, was crucial as a basis for development economics of many schools and opinions. Even those who think the right macroeconomic policy is to remove market distortions and help to create the infrastructure for an efficient functioning of the market, and who consider themselves as Keynesians and question the need for a separate 'development economics'[3] would still share in this general Keynesian objective to make economic reality conform more closely to the economic potential. In fact, the very concept of 'underdevelopment' or the need for 'development' embodies this objective. It is more a matter of priorities. For Keynes, in the conditions of the United Kingdom in the 1930s, with intolerable unemployment and other unutilised capacities, to stimulate the potential seemed more important than resource allocation through markets and prices or X-efficiency. Many development economists would accept Keynes' ranking; the anti-Keynesians do not. But most would not question that macroeconomic management is also important, as Keynes did not question the importance of allocation and business management.

(b) Directly, in so far as this put the emphasis on the utilisation of unemployed (and by extension underemployed) resources, and specifically human resources, as a source of economic growth and welfare. These became crucial concepts in the thinking and policy prescriptions for LDCs foreshadowing employment-oriented and basic needs-oriented development strategies as well as the Lewis surplus labour model and the Nurske balanced growth model.

(c) Indirectly, in so far as the maintenance of full employment by the major industrial countries would sustain commodity prices (Keynes was throughout an ardent advocate of stabilised primary commodity prices)[4] and also because the sustained demand from the industrial countries would make it possible and safe for LDCs to expand by Keynesian policies without coming up too soon against a foreign exchange constraint and domestic inflationary pressures.

The concept of duo-economics, i.e. that circumstances alter not only cases but also economics, was subsequently applied to other important distinctions. For instance Prebisch, Seers and others applied it to the distinction between the centre and the periphery when it became the basis of the dependency theories. The Prebisch–Singer hypothesis of deteriorating terms of trade is based on a similar distinction between exporters of primary commodities as against exporters of manufactured goods. Arthur Lewis in his model of economic development started with a Keynesian distinction between situations of unlimited supplies of labour *versus* situations when the rural labour surplus is exhausted (although he then reluctantly abandoned the Keynesian framework as not directly applicable to LDCs).[5] Other extensions of duo-economics which have become important for development analysis include the distinction between countries which are technical innovators and derive monopoly rents from this capacity as against countries incapable of technological innovation; here Keynesian duo-economics is combined with a Schumpeterian type of analysis. Yet another important distinction was that between capital surplus countries which are investors and creditors as against countries which depend on borrowing and receipt of investments. In all these ways Keynes' methodological move from monoeconomics to duo-economics as defined by Hirschman has been of the highest possible relevance not only analytically for development economics, but also politically in suggesting policies for LDCs.

Keynes was of course not thinking of the LDCs when he wrote the *General Theory* and advocated full employment for the industrial countries, or more specifically for the United Kingdom of 1936. On the contrary, he showed no interest in their problems and never visited any LDCs (not even India, even though his first book was devoted to Indian currency problems). In fact, he was then quite ready to maintain his full-employment policy by such means as a revenue tariff or other protective measures as might be necessary in the chaotic conditions and breakdown of the world economic order in the 1930s, even though such measures would have prevented a spread of the benefits of full employment policies to other countries, including the LDCs. But there are two important qualifications, i.e. (a) Keynes' advocacy of stabilised commodity prices and (b) the fact that many LDCs were then within the currency and revenue system of the British Empire. Keynes' readiness to accept protection as an instrument of full employment was also directly influential in inducing a number of development economists, e.g. Prebisch and the Economic Commission for Latin America (ECLA), to advocate protection as part of import substitution as a strategy for initiating industrialisation (although the parentage for this can be traced much beyond Keynes to Hamilton's and List's infant industries).

Another direction in which Keynes' overall philosophy and methodology is directly applicable to LDCs lies in his belief and vision that the limits to economic growth and welfare need not be set by financial resources but only by the availability of real resources. Where these exist the job of finance is simply to mobilise and employ the available and potential real resources in the most effective way. In this way, as Keynes himself put it, proper economic management and proper use of finance can perform the miracle of turning stone into bread. That is not a bad definition of the task of development itself. Development is exactly such a 'miracle' as described by Keynes; there are plenty of stones around in the form of unutilised and under-utilised actual and potential resources and the job is to turn the useless stones of unused potential into the bread of development.

The broad philosophy of the *General Theory* can be - and has been - described as combining macroeconomic management, which is the responsibility of the government (in Keynes' case, the maintenance of effective demand sufficient to create and maintain full employment) with microeconomic liberalism. In

Keynes' system once the macroeconomic management is on the right lines there is no further need for much micro management. The job is not to abolish markets but to manipulate them so that they yield the right results in terms of full employment. Now this prescription of effective, and if necessary tight, macro management which then makes it possible to utilise liberal market forces is exactly what is being preached today to LDCs, although 'in reverse' as it were – in the name of adjustment and restraint rather than expansion and full employment.

Certainly Indian development planning was from the very beginning inspired by such macroeconomic Keynesian concepts, filtered through to India through V.K.R.V. Rao and P.C. Mahalanobis. It is no accident that the latter, the father of Indian development planning, in the 'Mahalanobis model', closely followed the Keynesian national income analysis and used, or rather anticipated, a version of the Harrod–Domar model which also was directly derived from Keynesian categories, as developed by Colin Clark. It can of course be objected that Rao and Mahalanobis adopted only half of the Keynesian prescription, i.e. the macroeconomic management, but not the micro-liberalism. That is certainly true and, with the benefit of hindsight, India might have fared better with a closer approach to the full Keynesian mixture. On the other hand, both Rao and Mahalanobis were well aware of the limits of relevance for the conditions of India of Keynesian thinking in respect of micro-liberalism. The effective markets, response to price incentives and availability of complementary unused resources, in addition to unemployed labour, close linkages and high multipliers, could be assumed (or rather taken for granted) by Keynes; but they could certainly not be assumed for India, as Rao clearly pointed out in his key article on 'Investment, Income and the Multiplier in an Underdeveloped Economy'.[6]

On the other hand, it can be objected – and is now fashionable to argue – that the Keynesian idea of macroeconomic management also presupposed the existence of data, institutions and administrative capacity which Keynes took for granted for the United Kingdom of 1936, whereas they are conspicuously absent in the case of many LDCs. But surely the right approach then would not be to abandon the idea of macroeconomic management but to create the data, institutions, and administrative capacity which can make it possible and effective. One could add that even in the case of the United Kingdom, Keynes was highly conscious of the absence of the necessary data infrastructure and the need to create one – hence his interest in national income statistics and his inspiration of Colin Clark for his pioneer work on national income statistics.

Over the many discussions whether macroeconomic policy should be 'Keynesian' or 'monetarist' or 'neutral', or whether its objective should be growth or control of inflation or reduction of unemployment or relief of poverty or balance-of-payments equilibrium (or rather what weight should be given to these various objectives) – over all these debates we are in danger of forgetting that the very idea of macroeconomic policy is a legacy of the Keynesian revolution. In that sense even the 'anti-Keynesians' are part of the Keynesian legacy without realising it – demonstrating Keynes' own insight, in the last chapter of the *General Theory* that 'practical men, who believe themselves to be quite exempt from any intellectual influences, are usually the slaves of some defunct economist'.[7] Even a negative or passive or neutral macroeconomic policy is still a macroeconomic policy. 'There is no sense in which governments can abstain from having a macroeconomic policy; the only question is what macroeconomic policy it is.'[8]

What the anti-Keynesians accuse Keynesianism of doing is of exaggerating the need for government intervention and ignoring its dangers to the extent of creating 'dirigiste dogma'.[9] That criticism is not perhaps applied less to Keynes himself than to his followers; since Keynes was thinking of the British economy in the 1930s he did in fact assume reasonably functioning markets and high supply elasticities. His macroeconomic planning was essentially limited to establishing the macroeconomic framework within which microeconomic choice could be rationally made. It was more those who tried to apply Keynes to the conditions of developing countries who argued that given the institutional and supply rigidities of developing countries and

the scarcity of private entrepreneurship, government intervention should not be limited to the macroeconomic framework,
but should also extend to the supply side of the economy,
helping to break bottlenecks and replacing the non-existent
market mechanism through public enterprise or specific incentives. Yet Keynes is often held responsible by the anti-Keynesians
for having opened the flood gates to the 'dirigiste dogma' by
introducing the idea that without a proper macroeconomic
environment markets may well produce the stagnation of
'underemployment equilibrium'. The anti-Keynesian position is
that 'getting prices right' will by itself create a macroeconomic
climate or framework for growth and development; whereas the
Keynesian position is that 'getting prices right' only makes sense
and leads to growth and development after the macroeconomic
framework has been established. Or in the words of John
Toye:

> The correction of one error must not be allowed to be the
> opportunity for the introduction of an equal and opposite
> error. The neoclassicals have done well to insist that the
> development economist cannot make macroeconomic tech-
> niques substitute for microeconomic. But equally, the sub-
> stitution of microeconomic for macroeconomic is not
> possible. Although both types of techniques are inherently
> limited, they can and should be used concordantly.[10]

It is part of the anti-Keynesian attack on the 'dirigiste dogma' to
argue that the success stories in economic development are
characterised by lack of intervention whereas the failures are
identified with excessive government planning. However, the
empirical basis for this allegation is very weak, as has been shown
convincingly by Amartya Sen.[11] Among his success stories are
China, Yugoslavia, Romania, Sri Lanka, South Korea and
Taiwan, all of which show strong government interventions.
Around the last two countries, i.e. Korea and Taiwan, the anti-
Keynesians have created a myth that these are free market
economies, and that their economic success is essentially due to
their capacity to 'get prices right'. Although this myth has been

exploded by more careful empirical work, it dies hard. In fact both Korea and Taiwan are examples of strong and detailed government intervention, by no means limited to the macro-economic framework.[12] The anti-Keynesian argument often comes very close to a tautology: successful government intervention is declared to be successful, because it got prices right and relied on market incentives, and vice versa for unsuccessful intervention. Intervention which got prices right is non-dirigiste, and not really 'intervention'. Hence intervention is bad and the great advocate of intervention, Keynes, must be a bad influence.

Where the limits of Keynes' relevance are reached, and especially in relation to LDCs, is in his concentration on the demand side of macro management. From the very beginning, many of the doubts about the relevance of Keynesianism for LDCs have concentrated on the supply bottlenecks for human and technological as well as physical capital and other supply and institutional 'structural rigidities' in LDCs.[13] On the other hand, the emphasis of the Keynesian system on the rate of investment as a crucial instrument of policy – subsequently singled out in the Harrod–Domar model – played a great part in making Keynes' thinking influential in LDCs, well beyond the mere methodology of macroeconomic management to achieve desired objectives and its frame of reference in national income analysis. Even if it is accepted that macroeconomic policy in LDCs must pay special attention, and put greater emphasis, on developing the supply side of the economy and removing obstacles on the supply side, that does not in itself fall outside the Keynesian methodology of governmental macro-intervention. That would only be the case if we assumed *either* that government policy cannot make any difference to real supply *or* that governments are intrinsically incapable of following the right supply-side oriented macro-policies. While some of the rhetoric from monetarist quarters may come close to such a position, we may note that if this view were really held seriously by such 'conservative' institutions as the IMF, there would be no point in IMF missions, recommendations and conditions addressed inevitably to governments especially in view of IMF emphasis on the sovereignty of advised governments to use their own priorities in choosing the instruments and sectors by which to implement agreed macro-policies.[14]

There is an interesting parallel, in the current 'summit' discussion among the Western OECD countries, to the centre/periphery duo-economics inspired by Keynes, with greater emphasis on supply 'rigidities' in the less developed (periphery) part. Within the OECD context, the United States represents the 'centre' and Europe the 'periphery'. It is very noticeable that in the United States the emphasis is on Keynesian demand management, deficit financing and broad-based expansion with significant reductions of unemployment, whereas in the European countries the failure to match United States expansion is attributed to the greater structural 'rigidities' of European economies and macroeconomic policies are to be weighted on the side of removing such rigidities, e.g. in labour markets and introduction of new technology, rather than simple demand expansion.[15]

If we agree for the moment that the essential path to development is to increase supply rather than effective demand, this does not make the Keynesian emphasis on increasing investment irrelevant. Rather, it tells us something about the nature and composition of that investment. It must be directed purposefully towards the breaking of bottlenecks in supply.[16] A poor country cannot afford investment 'digging holes and filling them up again', simply to break the deadlock of unemployment equilibrium and set the multiplier to work. Nor can it afford overall investment to generate 'balanced growth', because even though such investment would generate its own savings it would not generate its own foreign exchange nor would it in fact generate 'balanced growth' where there are bottlenecks in supply.[17] While the former constraint applies only to balance-of-payments deficit countries (i.e. not to some oil exporters and some export successes), the latter is generic to developing countries. It is one of their characteristics, almost by definition, not only that there are supply bottlenecks but also that they lack the technological capacity to break them easily. Hence the recipe of 'unbalanced growth' is more relevant, at least in the sense of investment purposefully concentrated on the breaking of supply bottlenecks.[18] Selectivity of investment has to be added to the volume of investment emphasised by Keynes.

Food supply being an important bottleneck and key constraint on growth and full employment nearly everywhere in the LDCs, this is a clear priority for investment. Another equally widespread constraint is the foreign exchange shortage, hence priority for export generating and import saving investment. Where food is imported, as it is now in the majority of developing countries, the two priorities coincide and there is usually a top priority here for investment. Even the IMF and World Bank economists, with all their fanatical belief in the superiority of export-orientation over import substitution, will concede a major exception for the domestic production of imported food. From the point of view of assessing the relevance of Keynes for LDCs the important point is that the role of investment-led growth remains valid whether the main constraint is on the demand side or supply side. And let us remember that Amartya Sen has taught us that the food bottleneck in developing countries, even in the extreme cases of famine, is as much or more a matter of 'entitlement', i.e. of income and access through effective demand, as of supply.[19] This represents, in our context, a reinstatement of Keynesianism over the 'supply-side' arguments dating back to Rao, questioning Keynes' relevance.[20]

In developing countries, the expansion of agricultural and food production which is a precondition for expanded employment and expanded demand there is not just a matter of the normal economic elasticities of supply with which the Keynesian analysis operates. Rather it is strongly a question of structural changes, of land reform, changes in land tenure, relations between farmers and traders as well as money lenders, agricultural credit systems, extensions systems, and so on. As Michal Kalecki has put it, compared with such necessary structural and political factors the Keynesian policies of demand management amount to a mere 'financial trick'. 'It is perfectly clear', he writes 'that overcoming the resistance to such institutional changes by the privileged classes is a much more difficult proposition than the financial trick which solves the problem of effective demand crucial to the developed economies.'[21] Kalecki goes on to add the need for adequate taxation of the rich and well-to-do to make room for higher investments as another of the structural and political preconditions for application of Keynesian policies in developing countries without excessive inflation. He rightly points out that this political problem as well as the more administrative problems of tax collection and tax evasion are assumed away or taken for granted in the Keynesian system.[22]

When pointing out that the foreign exchange gap prevents the application of Keynesian expansionist policies in developing countries, it is of course essential to add that if Keynes' proposals, worked out in London during the war and vainly fought for by him at Bretton Woods, for a new financial and monetary world system suitable for a Keynesian global economy had prevailed, the foreign exchange constraint would not be so fatal. The reference here is to Keynes' proposals, at various times and under various names, for a world central bank, for a world currency, for automatic liquidity, for stable commodity prices, and generally for a world system in which the pressure for adjustment, at times of global unemployment, would be on the balance-of-payments surplus countries rather than the deficit countries. What a contrast to what we actually got! As long as full employment was pursued and achieved in the major industrial countries, the difference between what Keynes wanted and what we got was not so obvious and not so important; this happy coincidence gave us twenty-five 'golden years' of non-inflationary growth in the world, with much of it trickling down to the developing countries. The contrast with today is only too painfully obvious. If today it seems almost cynical to ask about the relevance of Keynes in relation to developing countries struggling under big balance-of-payments deficits and debt burdens, and expected to adjust unilaterally, the reason is not so much an irrelevance of

Keynesian policies but rather the abandonment of the objectives for which the Keynesian system was designed. If control of inflation, debt repayment and restoration of balance-of-payments equilibrium displace growth, employment and reduction of poverty as the chief objectives, it is not surprising that the Keynesian policies appear inapplicable.

But even in its apparent defeat, Keynesian thinking still scores an intellectual triumph. The triumph consists in the fact that those now pursuing what they imagine to be monetarist and anti-Keynesian objectives, still employ the Keynesian technique of demand management. The present IMF policies are in fact Keynesian in that they are based on demand management. But if they represent Keynesianism, it is Keynesianism in reverse.It is restrictive and deflationary demand management rather than expansionist demand management, but demand management all the same. Moreover, like all the rest of us, the so-called anti-Keynesians or neo-classicals employ the Keynesian categories of thinking in terms of macro-economic management of investment, saving, consumption, GNP, GDP, etc. Another lip service paid to Keynesianism in current adjustment policy making symbolised by the IMF is that the justification for restriction, control of inflation, devaluation, cuts in government expenditure, etc. is that this will then lay the foundation for subsequent 'sound sustainable growth'. So, whatever credibility may attach to this, even the anti-Keynesians hold out the promise of resumed Keynesianism some time in the future. One can have one's doubt whether in many cases the restrictions now enforced, particularly in social government expenditures, do not in fact destroy the chances of subsequent growth,[23] but at least the justification for what is being done to destroy and oppose Keynesian approaches is that this is only a transitional phase. In fact, this standard IMF argument subscribes to the Keynesian view that circumstances not only alter cases but also fundamental economics.

The chief anti-Keynesian of course was F.A. Hayek. His doctrine was that market solutions to economic and social problems are inherently superior to government solutions. This is because the knowledge available to a central bureaucracy can never match the knowledge disbursed through a market; centralised decision-making by governments lays the economy open to the risk of big mistakes while decentralised decision-making through the market avoids or minimises this risk; and only the market is truly democratic because it acknowledges the sovereignty of the individual consumer and buyer. Is this Hayekian anti-Keynesiansim more relevant for developing countries than Keynes? This is a difficult question to answer. Hayek, and following him Lal and Bauer, would argue that governments in developing countries have even less knowledge and less data for rational intervention than in developed countries; that they are also often less democratic and reflect the interests of the community less than democratically elected governments in industrial countries; that they are more likely to make big mistakes because their motives and objectives are often not the Keynesian objectives of growth with redistribution through full employment. On the other hand, Keynesians could argue that the market system in developing countries is also less free, less knowledgeable, less capable of rational decision making, less organised for getting signals from the consumer and final buyer and even when getting the signals, less capable of responding to them.

Both these positions have obvious elements of truth, and where you draw the balance may be more a matter of ideology and subjective judgement than of economic analysis. If you have a United Nations – accepting governments as the sovereign representatives of the interests of their respective countries; if you give much weight to the imperfections of the private market; if you emphasise the role which government expenditure can play in providing the infrastructure now missing to make private markets effective, you will be a Keynesian and think of Keynes being relevant. If you hold the reverse opinions and put weight on the wickedness and inefficiencies of governments while playing down those of the private sector, you will be an anti-Keynesian in relation to developing countries. It would be quite possible, logically, to be a Keynesian for some developing countries and an anti-Keynesian for others. Obviously the developing countries are not homogeneous when it comes to working out the crucial ratio of governmental deficiencies to private market deficiencies. While this does not take us very far in terms of economic analysis, it does help us to understand both the passion and the inconclusiveness of the current debate on the relevance of Keynes to developing countries.

The current situation in the developing countries in one sense underlines the relevance of Keynesianism for developing countries, and yet at the same time it also shows up its limitations. In many developing countries, whether as the natural result of the world recession or whether as a result of restrictive policies imposed by the IMF there is at present widespread under-utilised capacity of capital as well as of labour. In some of the African countries, e.g. Zambia, the great bulk of productive capacity for manufactured consumption goods and simple capital goods lies idle, and has done so for years, while there is clearly a heavy volume of unemployed and underemployed labour. At the same time the better utilisation of existing capacity is an essential principal condition also for agricultural revival. Agricultural output is held back more than anything else by the absence of the simple manufactured goods which the farmers need to induce them to produce surpluses for sale, such as blankets, soap, clothing, shoes and radios. For all of these the productive capacity is there. The same applies to manufactured inputs such as fertiliser, pesticides, agricultural tools and equipment. This is an ideal situation for the application of Keynesian principles; there are plenty of stones around to be turned into bread (literally) by the magic of finance, through the application of Keynesian multipliers and Nurksean balanced growth.

The trouble, of course, is that the 'finance' which is needed to turn the stones into bread for developing countries today is not domestic finance but foreign exchange. The reason why the capacity is idle is that the foreign exchange is not there to import the necessary spare parts, raw materials, expertise, etc. which would be needed to set the idle equipment to work. Similarly, it is balance-of-payments difficulties and lack of foreign exchange which has forced the developing countries into restrictive anti-Keynesian policies. So the present situation, although in one sense ideal ground for the application of Keynesianism, shows that it is the Keynes II, the Keynes of Bretton Woods, who is relevant rather than the Keynes I of the *General Theory*. If Keynes' ideas had prevailed at Bretton Woods, if we had global demand management, a world central bank, automatic liquidity, mobilisation of balance-of-payments surpluses, symmetric adjustment policies not bearing unilaterally upon the deficit countries, a world currency based on, for example, stabilised commodity prices, this kind of global Keynesianism would be our salvation today. It is the balance-of-payments surpluses of Japan today (and, of course, also those of Kuwait, Libya, Saudi Arabia and West Germany) which ought to supply the Keynesian finance not only to restart growth and development in the developing countries, but also to reduce unemployment and utilise the widespread idle capacity in so many of the industrialised countries as well. If only. . . !

Let us remember sadly that initially at Bretton Woods, not only Keynes, but even Harry Dexter White at first proposed an International Development Board and Inter-Allied Bank respectively. Both were designed for the development of the world economy as a whole. The World Bank which finally emerged from Bretton Woods was 'barely a pale shadow' of those original plans.[24] It is also of interest to note that in the Bretton Woods discussion, especially in relation to the Articles of Agreement of the IMF and definition of its purposes, the debate on the relevance or non-relevance of Keynes to developing countries erupted quite sharply. The original draft established the objective of the 'maintenance of a high level of employment and real income'. But the Indian delegation argued throughout that these Keynesian concepts had little meaning in the context of India and asked that the draft be amended to reflect the different conditions of developing countries. After a continued debate throughout the Bretton Woods conference, as a final compromise the notion of 'maintenance' of employment and income was broadened to include *'promotion and* maintenance'. Furthermore, the 'development of the productive resources of all members' was added as an objective of expanded international trade. Even so one wonders whether the Indian delegation would have been satisfied with this more direct application of Keynesian concepts to developing countries (on the lines of the dynamisation of Keynes by the Harrod-Domar formula) if they had realised that the International Trade Organisation, the essential third leg of the Bretton Woods trio, would fail to be created, thus leaving primary commodity exporters without the protection of global stabilisation measures.

It has repeatedly emerged in this essay that Keynes' relevance for developing countries can only be judged by taking into account the international Keynes II as well as the domestic Keynes I. There is a clear logical relationship in this extension. The domestic Keynes I of the 1936 *General Theory* pointed out that the micro decisions made by individual firms and individual workers and consumers based upon their own micro profit/loss calculations did not usually result in a macro optimum for the whole economy. He then described the corrective action that would be needed to reconcile the two. In the same way he based his approach to the management of the world economy on the view that the action taken by individual countries at what is from a global point of view a micro level in their own national interests and according to their own lights and conditions may not lead to a global optimum. He then described the corrective action needed and the framework and policy instruments for this corrective action. Unfortunately his view did not prevail, and even the application of the truncated Bretton Woods system has sadly deteriorated in the recent past. We now have the sad spectacle of an IMF which operates on an *ad hoc* basis, country by country and with insufficient resources on a restrictive basis, and in the balance-of-payments deficit countries exclusively, with predictable unfortunate results for the global economy. 'All too often such policies amount to a mere suppression of growth, damaging future development projects rather than promoting them.'[25] The way pointed to by Keynes II was the better way. Let us hope that we can get back to it, before it is too late.

COMMENT

The author has dealt with the general subject of this contribution on other occasions, for example in 'The Relevance of Keynes for Developing Countries', *Estudos de Economia*, Vol. IV, No. 4, July-September 1984, pp. 419–38 and in *The Policy Consequences of John Maynard Keynes* (ed. Arnold Tovell), M.E. Sharpe, New York, 1985. The present contribution represents a further development of his thinking on the subject. The paper here was invited and not delivered at the Seminar – Editor.

NOTES

1. Keynes, J.M. (1936) *The General Theory of Employment, Interest and Money* (London: Macmillan), Henceforth referred to as *General Theory*.
2. Hirschman, A.O. (1982) 'The Rise and Decline of Development Economics', contribution to *The Theory and Experience of Economic Development: Essays in Honor of Sir W. Arthur Lewis*, M. Gersovitz *et al.* (eds) (London: George Allen and Unwin).
3. Such as Deepak Lal (1983) *The Poverty of Development Economics* (London: Institute of Economic Affairs), and P.T. Bauer (1984) *Reality and Rhetoric: Studies in the Economics of Development* (London: Weidenfeld and Nicolson).
4. Keynes, J.M. (1983) 'The Policy of Government Storage of Foodstuffs and Raw Materials', *Economic Journal*, September, 38 pp 449–60.
5. Lewis, W.A. (1954) 'Economic Development with Unlimited Supplies of Labour', *The Manchester School*. May, pp. 139–91.
6. Rao, V.K.R.V. (1952) 'Investment, Income and the Multiplier in an Underdeveloped Economy', *The Indian Economic Review*, February.
7. *General Theory*, p. 383. Perhaps we may add 'and women' after men!
8. Stewart, M. (1983) *Controlling the Economic Future – Policy Dilemmas in a Shrinking World* (Brighton: Harvester Press, p. 13).
9. This term is the one used by Deepak Lal, loc. cit.
10. Toye, J. (1985) 'Dirigisme and development economics', *Cambridge Journal of Economics*, 9, pp. 1–14.
11. Sen, A.K. (1983) 'Development, which way now?', *Economic Journal*, December, pp. 745–62.

88   KEYNES AND ECONOMIC DEVELOPMENT

12. For Korea, see for example Richard Luedde-Neurath, 'State interventior
    and foreign direct investment in South Korea', *IDS Bulletin*, Vol. 15, No. 2
    pp. 18–25. For Taiwan, see Robert Wade, 'Dirigisme Taiwan-style', *IDS*
    Bulletin, Vol. 15, No. 2. For Korea see also H.W. Singer (1984) 'Indus-
    trialisation. Where do we stand? Where are we going?' *Industry and Develop-
    ment*, No. 12, UNIDO, pp. 79–87; and Paul Streeten (1985) 'A problem to
    every solution', *Finance and Development*, June, Vol. 22, No. 2, pp. 14–16.
13. For example, V.K.R.V. Rao, loc. cit.
14. As Mr. De Larosière, the Executive Director of the IMF, declared in a
    recent pamphlet: 'An international institution such as the Fund canno
    take upon itself the role of dictating social and political objectives to
    sovereign governments.' (*Does the Fund Impose Austerity?* Washington: IMF
    June 1984.)
15. During the discussions at the recent Bonn summit of the Western 'Big
    Seven', 'President Reagan told his colleagues he was doing everything
    possible to reduce the US budget deficit and the Europeans in turn ben
    over backwards to tell the Americans they were trying to reduce structura
    rigidities in their economies and become as flexible as the Americans.' (*The
    Observer*, 5 May 1985.)
16. This conclusion is also reached by A.P. Thirlwall when discussing 'Th
    Keynesian approach to the finance of development'. See *Growth and
    Development, with special reference to developing countries* (London: Macmillan
    Third edition, 1983, p. 274).
17. This is a slightly different version of Chenery's 'two gaps'. Chenery's
    savings gap prejudges the Keynesian view that savings can be generated by
    investment. The supply gap seems a more relevant formulation.
18. This, of course, comes close to the position of Hirschman in *The Strategy of
    Economic Development* (New Haven, Conn.: Yale, 1958).
19. Sen, A.K. (1981) *Poverty and Famines: an essay on entitlement and deprivation*
    (Oxford: Clarendon).
20. Rao, V.K.R.V., loc. cit.
21. Kalecki, M. (1976) *Essays on Developing Economies* (Brighton: Harvester Press
    p. 26. This paper represents an address given by Kalecki at the Reunion o
    Latin American Schools of Economics, Mexico City, June 1965. It doe
    not, therefore, represent one of the early Kaleckian writings pre-dating
    Keynes, and it may thus be taken as a direct reference to the Keynesian
    'financial tricks' of the *General Theory*. Keynesian policies were of course ir
    full and successful application in the industrial countries in 1965.
22. Ibid.
23. This is argued for example in *The Impact of World Recession on Children*, a
    study prepared for UNICEF, edited by Richard Jolly and Andrea Cornia
    (Oxford: Pergamon Press, 1984) and also in a special issue of *World Develop-
    ment*, Vol. 12, No. 3, March 1984.
24. This term is used by J.G. Ruggie in 'Political Structure and Change in the
    International Economic Order: The North–South Dimension', *The
    Antinomies of Interdependence, National Welfare and the International Division o
    Labor* (New York: Columbia University Press, 1983) p. 430. See also there
    for further discussion of the matters discussed in this paragraph.

25. This statement comes from the report of the United Nations Committee for Development Planning Working Group on Review and Appraisal of Implementation of the International Development Strategy in accordance with paragraph 8 of General Assembly resolution 37/202 of 20 December 1982, A/AC.219/21 of 19 April 1984, para. 33.

Session 2

INTRODUCTION I
M.J.C. Vile (Chairman)

In this second session, we turn to matters explicitly international in scope. If the Keynes plan had been adopted at Bretton Woods instead of the White Plan, a World Central Bank would have been established with the power to create international money to use for collectively agreed purposes, such as development assistance for developing countries particularly, perhaps, to cope with debt difficulties and commodity price fluctuations. To give the first paper we are very fortunate to have Dr John Williamson of the highly respected and influential Institute for International Economics in Washington. Dr Williamson is an expert on international economic issues, and is well known for his various proposals for international monetary reform. Before the breakdown of Bretton Woods, he was a leading advocate of the 'crawling peg' system of exchange rate adjustment, and in recent years, since the breakdown of Bretton Woods, he has been an advocate of target zones for exchange rates to replace the chaos of freely floating rates. He is the author of such books as *The Failure of World Monetary Reform; The Open Economy and the World Economy*, and, more recently, *The Exchange Rate System*. He will discuss this afternoon the difference that the Keynes plan might have made to developing countries since the war had it been adopted.

BANCOR AND THE DEVELOPING COUNTRIES:
HOW MUCH DIFFERENCE WOULD IT HAVE MADE?
John Williamson

Suppose that the British proposals for an International Clearing Union (ICU) had received such an ecstatic Congressional reception in April 1943 that Harry Dexter White and the United States Treasury had felt obliged to abandon their modest counter-proposals for a stabilisation fund and to endorse the Keynes Plan instead. Suppose also that the ICU in the form in which it was envisaged by Keynes had withstood the test of time and survived essentially intact to 1985. (As will be found below, my credulity is strained beyond breaking point by supposing that it could have survived without any modifications at all.) How different would the position and prospects of the developing countries be today?

My answer to this question will suppose that the post-war international monetary system had been based on the Keynes Plan as presented in the White Paper of April 1943, reproduced in Horsefield (1969, pp. 19–36) and in the appendix to this volume. The relevant paragraphs are cited in parentheses. My interpretation of paragraphs 21–22 may be constroversial and is justified in the appendix to this paper.

The key features of the Keynes Plan were:

(a) An international monetary unit called bancor (paragraphs 4, 27).
(b) An adjustable peg par value system in which all countries declared par values in terms of bancor, and undertook to convert balances of their currency needed to make current account payments into the currency of any other member at parity[1] (paragraphs 6 (3), 6 (8)).

(c) The centralised clearing of foreign exchange transactions with each central bank and among the central banks in the ICU (paragraphs 21-2).

(d) Exchange controls over capital transactions in all member countries (paragraphs 32-3).

(e) The creation of rights to overdraw bancor balances in the ICU, by up to 25 per cent of the total overdraft limit in any year or more with special permission (paragraph 6(8) (a)).

(f) Automatic increases in the size of those overdraft rights in accordance with the growth in the nominal value of world trade, to maintain them equal to 75 per cent of the average value of trade over the preceding five years (paragraph 6(5)).

(g) An unlimited obligation to accept bancor in settlement of balance of payments surpluses (paragraphs 6(6), 8).

(h) Penalties in the form of an interest charge of 1 (2) per cent on both excessive use of overdraft facilities and excessive accumulation of bancor balances, where excess is defined as more than 25 per cent (50 per cent) of the size of overdraft limits, hereafter called 'quotas' (paragraph 6(7)).

(i) A once-for-all right for countries with debit balances exceeding one quarter of their quota to depreciate by up to 5 per cent within a year (paragraph 6(8) (a)), and the right of the Governing Board of the ICU to order reductions in the par values of countries with debit balances exceeding one half of quota (paragraph 6(8) (b)).

THE EXCHANGE RATE SYSTEM

The Keynes Plan incorporated a par value system. This might have survived to the present day in the context of comprehensive adoption of the Keynes Plan, since (a) this incorporated the general maintenance of exchange controls over capital transactions; and (b) the availability of an alternative reserve asset, bancor, might have avoided the development of a reserve role for the dollar and this might have made the United States more willing to change its par value in a timely way. Despite these factors, my own guess is that the system would nonetheless have broken down unless the major powers had agreed to limit the size of exchange rate changes (i.e. move to a crawling peg) at a relatively early date.

Unless it had been operated in an extremely foolish way (which is not inconceivable, given the relatively weak disciplining role of speculative capital flows limited to leads and lags because of exchange controls), a par value system among the major currencies would have been helpful to the developing countries. Such a system would have avoided the dilemma they currently face in choosing between pegging to a single currency and risking having their macroeconomic policy thrown into disarray by a movement of the peg currency against all others, or pegging to a currency composite and losing any firm anchor to an international currency in which they can invoice, cover, borrow, and hold assets. It would have prevented their dollar-denominated debts being magnified relative to their export earning potential by a vast appreciation of the dollar such as occurred in 1980–85. And it should have limited the protectionist pressures that have been generated by currency misalignments. Thus, even without claiming credit for the better coordination of macroeconomic policy among the major countries that some of us believe a par value system tends to induce (Williamson, 1985), there are ample reasons for believing that the developing countries would have benefited from retention of a par value system.

CENTRALISED EXCHANGE TRANSACTIONS

As argued in the appendix to this paper, Keynes envisaged the centralisation of all exchange transactions through central banks followed by the clearing of their net balances with the ICU. This is a radically different arrangement to the competitive exchange markets that re-emerged in the post-war world.

One advantage of this arrangement, as Keynes perceived it, was that it would have facilitated the operation of capital controls. But provided that it were combined with a general open licence for imports (including invisibles), centralised exchange clearing need not have been detrimental to trade transactions, unless centralised institutions are inherently less efficient than competitive markets. In fact, given how modest transaction costs are in the foreign exchange market, a centralised market would have to absorb several times as many resources as a competitive market in order for it to jeopardise the important benefits that the world economy unquestionably gained in the post-war period through liberal trade. Indeed, James Tobin (1984) has argued that financial markets have grown over-bloated, absorbing more resources than are needed to produce their real services, and tempting the public into short-sighted and socially inefficient speculation. It is at least possible that centralised foreign exchange trading would have limited such costs and left the public, including the developing countries, better off.

CAPITAL CONTROL

It is inconceivable that cross-border lending would have reached a fraction of its actual current level of over US$2 trillion (gross) by banks alone (principally in the Euro markets) under a regime of capital controls. Despite Keynes's longstanding hostility to foreign investment, there are undoubtedly important potential benefits from capital mobility: in shifting resources to areas where returns are higher; in permitting countries to anticipate, postpone, or smooth absorption relative to income; in enabling companies to exploit their technological or managerial expertise in additional markets; in diversifying risks; and in permitting mutually beneficial maturity transformation. At the same time, the tendency of the economics profession to assume that all capital movements must be explicable in terms of such benign motives, and therefore that free capital mobility is as presumptively Pareto optimal as free trade, can only be described as naive.

In fact, governments have borrowed to finance white

elephants as well as to make productive investments. They have borrowed to postpone adjustment and thereby have brought forward absorption to an excessive degree, as well as to avoid an unnecessary depression of output while necessary adjustment is in train. They have used transitory income to borrow and expand absorption even more, rather than saving in good times and borrowing in bad, as well as using the international capital market as a tool for living by the permanent income hypothesis. Many capital flows initiated by the private sector are of equally questionable benefit from a social standpoint: flows to avoid taxation, to seek speculative profits from exchange rate changes, to flee to 'safe havens'.

It is certainly possible, indeed likely, that under the Keynes Plan the developing countries would have been unable to borrow on the extensive scale that they did during the 1970s. Their growth would have suffered in consequence. But that loss would in my judgement have been outweighed by the benefit of avoiding the debt crisis.

BANCOR OVERDRAFT FACILITIES

The overdraft rights incorporated in the Keynes Plan were on a truly generous scale. Richard Gardner (1956, p. 87) states that they would have amounted to $26 billion at the outset, and they would have grown rapidly as world trade expanded and other countries joined the ICU. Europe would just about have been able to finance its post-war reconstruction by drawing on its overdraft facilities without any need for Marshall Aid.[2]

I calculated in 1983 that the scale of quotas envisaged by Keynes would have been equivalent to a once-for-all SDR allocation of over SDR 720 billion with no acceptance limit (Worswick and Trevithick, 1983, p. 93). Application of Keynes's formula to recent levels of trade would result in even larger figures, as shown in the table.

These are colossal magnitudes in comparison with international reserves (some $400 billion), let alone Fund-supplied reserves (some $58 billion). If the non-oil developing countries

TABLE 1   *Hypothetical ICU Quotas, 1985 (US$ billion)*

	Exports (1980–84 average)	Imports (1980–84 average)	Total trade	75% of trade
World	1,777	1,843	3,615	2,711
Oil-exporters	227	148	375	281
Non-oil developing countries	327	397	724	543

SOURCE   *International Financial Statistics.*

had available $543 billion in overdraft rights, one can be fairly confident that they would be using a good portion of them, even with a penal interest charge of 2 per cent. Perhaps a more potent deterrent to limit their use of these rights would have been the rights the ICU would have acquired to influence economic policies in heavily indebted countries. These were stated in the following terms in paragraph 6(8) of the Keynes Plan:

> (8) – (a) A member State may not increase its debit balance by more than a *quarter* of its quota within a year without the permission of the Governing Board. If its debit balance has exceeded a quarter of its quota on the average of at least two years, it shall be entitled to reduce the value of its currency in terms of bancor provided that the reduction shall not exceed 5 per cent without the consent of the Governing Board; but it shall not be entitled to repeat this procedure unless the Board is satisfied that this procedure is appropriate.
>
> (b) The Governing Board may require from a member State having a debit balance reaching a *half* of its quota the deposit of suitable collateral against its debit balance. Such collateral shall, at the discretion of the Governing Board, take the form of gold, foreign or domestic currency or government bonds, within the capacity of the member State. As a condition of allowing a member State to increase its debit balance to a figure in excess of a half of its quota, the Governing Board may require all or any of the following measures:
>
> (i) a stated reduction in the value of the member's currency, if it deems that to be the suitable remedy;

(ii) the control of outward capital transactions if not already in force; and

(iii) the outright surrender of a suitable proportion of any separate gold or other liquid reserve in reduction of its debit balance.

Furthermore, the Governing Board may recommend to the Government of the member State any internal measures affecting its domestic economy which may appear to be appropriate to restore the equilibrium of its international balance.

(c) If a member State's debit balance has exceeded *three-quarters* of its quota on the average of at least a year and is excessive in the opinion of the Governing Board in relation to the total debit balances outstanding on the books of the Clearing Union, or is increasing at an excessive rate, it may, in addition be asked by the Governing Board to take measures to improve its position, and, in the event of its failing to reduce its debit balance accordingly within two years, the Governing Board may declare that it is in default and no longer entitled to draw against its account except with the permission of the Governing Board.

With such provisions, it would seem likely that the average developing country would aim to use something under 50 per cent of its quota to secure a permanent resource transfer, and to use the difference between that and 75 per cent of its quota to fulfill the buffer-stock function that reserves perform under present arrangements. Suppose that they typically aimed to use about 40 per cent of their quotas. Then the bancor system would give a resource transfer of $217 billion to the non-oil developing countries, which would go over half way toward offsetting the virtual absence of bank lending (which currently approaches $400 billion). Furthermore, they would have effective reserves of the order of $190 billion (35 per cent of $543 billion–35 per cent being the difference between the uper limit of 75 per cent of quota and the 40 per cent norm), available without cost and increasing over time in line with the growth in their trade. These benefits would be substantial.

In fact, the benefits appear so substantial that one may doubt whether quotas could possibly have remained on the lavish scale envisaged by Keynes. Even before Bretton Woods he indicated an inclination to reduce their size somewhat: 'two-thirds [of exports plus imports] might perhaps be nearer the right figure than three-quarters' (JMK XXV, p. 246). Moreover, the Keynes Plan allowed the ICU to reduce overdraft limits if the threat of inflation materialised (paragraph 6 (13)). Judging by the experience of the IMF,[3] one may surmise that the world would have suffered a lot of inflation before this occurred, but that eventually the ICU would have got around to doing the necessary.

That it would have been necessary seems to me virtually certain. Countries have not typically restrained their spending to what was in their long-run interest except when constrained by an effective short-run liquidity constraint. Recall how many developing countries borrowed to excess when they achieved access to the international capital market in the 1970s. Or consider how Britain has gone out and spent a large part of the oil bonanza (on allowing unemployment to rise!) rather than setting the conscious aim of allowing consumption to increase by no more than permanent income, and saving the remainder. Again, think of the short-sighted folly that will shortly result in the United States becoming the world's leading debtor nation. Had policies been equally myopic and countries been as free of liquidity constraints as the Keynes Plan provided, the result could only hve been global inflation.

CONDITIONALITY

Keynes's ICU would have had both important similarities and important differences to the IMF as it functions today. The most important difference is that it would have provided a vastly larger scale of unconditional drawing rights. The first half of a member's quota would have been available unconditionally. Only when an overdraft reached 50 per cent of quota would the ICU have obtained the right to demand collateral or reimbursement, to require devaluation, or to recommend internal policy measures.

When an overdraft had exceeded 75 per cent of quota for a year, the ICU would have gained the additional right to require a member to take measures to improve its situation, on pain of being declared in default. At that point it would have exercised even stronger control over the full range of macroeconomic policies than the influence the IMF has over the policies of borrowing members. This similarity is hardly coincidental: it is an inevitable feature of a prudent lending institution that is precluded from following the traditional banker's maxim of lending only to those who do not really need the money. If one wishes to provide for a country to be able to borrow beyond the point that seems prudent to the lender, one has to allow the lender to insist on conditions that give it a reasonable expectation of recovering its money.[4]

Nor would the existence of conditionality have exhausted the similarities between Keynes's ICU and today's IMF. On the contrary, there can be little doubt that the measures invoked would have been similar in most crucial respects – for the compelling reason that their end object would have been the same, namely, to improve the balance of payments, and there is only limited scope for choice in how one sets about seeking that objective.

An improvement in the balance of payments almost invariably requires adjustment of the current account. The standard theory embodying the Keynesian tradition as synthesised by James Meade tells us that there are two major classes of instrument for improving the current account, namely expenditure reduction and expenditure switching. Expenditure reducing measures involving fiscal austerity and monetary contraction do indeed feature in most IMF Fund programmes, just as devaluation – the form of expenditure switching preferred by the Fund for compelling micro efficiency reasons – does. It could not be otherwise, because these are the measures that are relevant to the problem in hand. It would have been the same under Keynes's

ICU, which indeed provided quite explicitly for the ICU to be able to *require* a devaluation beyond a certain point. And the very fact that Keynes and his principal supporter, Roy Harrod, were so passionate to avoid arrangements that would compel *general* deflation because of a liquidity shortage, implies that they understood that this was an inevitable and appropriate element of the adjustment process when a country had gone excessively into debt.[5]

It is nonetheless reasonable to infer that there would have been two significant differences in the operation of conditionality between Keynes's ICU and today's IMF. The first relates to the *mix* in which expenditure reducing and expenditure switching policies were combined. One of the criticisms of the Fund to which I subscribe is the charge that a number of its programmes have involved excessive expenditure reduction ('overkill') involving the creation of substantial excess capacity and unemployment rather than just the elimination of excess demand and the liberation of resources in the non-tradable industries for redeployment into tradables. Conversely, in a number of African countries during the years of easy conditionality, 1979–81, the Fund seems to have required too little in the way of eliminating overvalued exchange rates. It does a country no service to lend it money without ensuring that it is taking the measures that will give it a good prospect of being able to repay without enduring even greater sacrifices than those avoided when the loan was made – yet this is essentially the situation of sub-Saharan Africa today. In this respect there is a strong presumption that Keynes's ICU would have operated differently to the way the IMF has done, because it would have had stronger powers to require devaluation (as soon as borrowing went over 50 per cent of quota), while its right to demand austerity would have started only when borrowing exceeded 75 per cent of quota. Indeed, the major objective of Keynes's proposals was always that of avoiding deflation in excess of what was essential, which makes it unlikely that the ICU would have engineered overkill like that experienced by Latin America since 1982. In my judgement, therefore, conditionality would have been materially improved under the ICU.

The second respect in which the ICU's conditions would have differed from those of the IMF relates to the capital account. It is mistaken to picture the IMF as insistent on the liberalisation of capital outflows. The convertibility requirement embodied in its Articles is explicitly limited to *current account* transactions. It is true that the Fund argues for realistic exchange rates and positive real interest rates as means of ending capital flight, but this is a reflection of realism rather than of an ideological commitment to *laissez-faire*: the Fund does not object to countries supplementing macroeconomic policy with capital controls. Nevertheless, this is a far cry from the ability that the ICU would have had to *require* a country with a debit balance in excess of 50 per cent of quota to introduce 'the control of outward capital transactions if not already in force' (paragraph 8 (b) (ii)). Had the post-war system maintained the general capital controls that Keynes favoured, capital controls would doubtless have remained a far more effective instrument than they are in the world today.

CONCLUSIONS

On the whole a world with an ICU would have provided more support to development than a world with the IMF. Capital controls would, it is true, have prevented the growth of a Eurodollar market and thus limited how much developing countries could borrow, but that would after all have avoided the debt crisis. Under Keynes's original formula the developing countries would in fact have been able to achieve a substantial resource transfer through the bancor system (though I have argued that such generous quotas would have been reduced long ago). In addition developing countries would have got a better exchange-rate system, access to reserves free of acquisition costs, and more appropriate conditionality.

At this moment in history it would be pointless to dream of putting the clock back to a world of capital immobility and centralised exchange transactions, or creating a bancor system to channel vast quantities of capital to developing countries. Fortunately Keynes's famous claim, 'the substitution of a credit mechanism in place of hoarding would have repeated in the international field the same miracle, already performed in the domestic field, of turning a stone into bread' (paragraph 12), was an exaggeration: a bancor system is neither necessary nor sufficient to keep the world economy close to full utilisation of its resources, which is the only sense I can make of his claim. Hopefully, it is less unrealistic to work for an improved exchange-rate system; for regular and substantial SDR allocations to avoid the outrageous anomaly whereby developing countries have to earn payments surpluses and help finance the United States budget deficit in order to build up their reserves; and for more appropriate conditionality.

APPENDIX: KEYNES AND THE CENTRALISATION OF EXCHANGE TRANSACTIONS

In my review of volumes XXV and XXVI of *The Collected Writings of John Maynard Keynes* (Williamson, 1981), I drew attention to Keynes's incorporation of centralised exchange transactions in his ICU. On re-examining the version of the Keynes Plan incorporated in the White Paper (which does not appear in one piece in volume XXV), I find that both paragraphs 21 and 22 explicitly deny such centralisation to be essential to the ICU:

21. The principles governing transactions are: first, that the Clearing Union is set up, not for the transaction of daily business between individual traders or banks, but for the clearing and settlement of the ultimate outstanding balances between Central Banks (and certain other super-national Institutions), such as would have been settled under the old gold standard by the shipment or the earmarking of gold, and should not trespass unnecessarily beyond this field; and, second, that its purpose is to increase *freedom* in international commerce and not to multiply interferences or compulsions.
22. Many Central Banks have found great advantage in centralising with themselves or with an Exchange Control the supply and demand of all foreign exchange, thus dispensing with an outside exchange market, though continuing to accommodate individuals through the existing banks and not directly. The further extension of such arrangements would be consonant with the general purposes of the Clearing Union, inasmuch as they would promote order and discipline in international exchange transactions in detail as well as in general. The same is true of the control of Capital

Movements, further described below, which many States are likely to wish to impose on their own nationals. But the structure of the proposed Clearing Union does not *require* such measures of centralisation or of control on the part of a member State. It is, for example, consistent alike with the type of Exchange Control now established in the United Kingdom or with the system now operating in the United States. The Union does not prevent private holdings of foreign currency or private dealings in exchange or international capital movements, if these have been approved or allowed by the member States concerned. Central Banks can deal direct with one another as heretofore. No transaction in bancor will take place except when a member State or its Central Bank is exercising the right to pay in it. In no case is there any direct control of capital movements by the Union, even in the case of 6 (8) (b) (ii) above, but only by the member States themselves through their own institutions. Thus the fabric of international banking organisation, built up by long experience to satisfy practical needs, would be left as undisturbed as possible.

Paragraph 22 was introduced at a late date prior to publication of the White Paper, between November 1942 and April 1943 (JMK XXV, appendix 3, p. 464). It might therefore have been a last-minute response to Dennis Robertson's protest 'Surely it is not true that CU assumes . . . a monopoly of exchange dealings on the part of every member state' (JMK XXV, p. 228), which had been provoked by Keynes's flat assertion, in comparing his ICU with White's Stabilisation Fund, that 'The CU presumes that member countries will operate an official monopoly of exchange transactions' (JMK XXV, p. 221). However, paragraph 21 goes back unchanged to a draft of January 1942 (JMK XXV, p. 125, paragraph 101), and appears equally clearly to deny the necessity of centralised exchange transactions (since there was no such centralisation under the gold standard).

Keynes's statements both before and after the White Paper (JMK XXV, p. 221 and XXVI, p. 123) leave no doubt that exchange centralisation was his preferred arrangement, and suggest that he normally thought of it as an integral element of his plan. Hence I have included it in my description of the Keynes Plan.

Nevertheless, it is interesting to ask whether the ICU could in fact have operated as Keynes envisaged *without* a monopoly of exchange transactions. The Keynes Plan stated that each central bank would buy and sell with the ICU at par (paragraph 4), but also that the ICU might (at its discretion) charge a small commission or transfer fee (paragraph 6 (6)). Presumably central banks would have posted a buying rate and a selling rate that were sufficiently far apart to cover their costs, including any commission that the ICU might have charged. Had buying and selling rates been sufficiently close together, there would have been no scope for private exchange markets (which arose under the gold standard because of the spread between the gold points and under Bretton Woods because of the 2 per cent band). A legal monopoly of foreign exchange would not have been necessary in order for the central bank to secure a *de facto* monopoly.

On the other hand, central banks could have set their buying and selling rates far enough apart to leave scope for the development of private exchange markets. Had member countries posted such rates in terms of the United States dollar, the microeconomics of the ICU would have differed little from those of the Bretton Woods system. The role of the Clearing Union would have been confined to clearing the net balances that arose from central bank intervention in the dollar market. Provided that central banks did in fact regularly clear their dollar acquisitions with the ICU, however, the development of a reserve currency system would have been avoided.

ACKNOWLEDGEMENT

The author acknowledges with gratitude comments by Robert Triffin on a previous draft.

NOTES

1. A parity is the ratio of two par values. As explained in the appendix, there would presumably have been some modest spread between the buying rate and the selling rate.
2. Although the United States would have earned interest (less penal interest charges for some years) on the finance that in the event it provided as Marshall aid, it would not necessarily have been better off as a result, if the ICU had in fact thwarted the emergence of the dollar's reserve role. According to Kolm (1970), seigniorage from use of the dollar as a reserve currency effectively compensated the United States for its expenditure on Marshall aid.
3. The outstanding examples concern the time taken to create the SDR, almost a decade from Triffin's *Gold and the Dollar Crisis* (1960) to the first allocations, and the agonising process of raising interest rates on Fund assets to realistic levels. When the General Arrangements to Borrow were founded, remuneration was set at an average of 1.5 per cent, half-way between the then prevailing interest rate of about 3 per cent and the zero interest rate on gold. This rate was subsequently applied to the SDR. When analysis pointed to the need for a commercial interest rate on the SDR, it was raised to 5 per cent (in June 1974), just halfway between 1.5 per cent and the prevailing rate of 8.5 per cent. It took two more adjustments before the gap was effectively closed. See Williamson (1977, p. 142).
4. The Keynes Plan (paragraph 16) stated explicitly: 'But if the purpose of the overdraft facilities is mainly to give time for adjustments, we have to make sure, so far as possible, that they *will* be made.' (Italics in original.)
5. In comparing his own proposals with those of White's Stabilisation Fund, Keynes stated that the provisions for disciplining debtor countries were 'substantially the same' (JMK XXV, p. 220).

REFERENCES

Gardner, Richard N. (1956) *Sterling-Dollar Diplomacy* (Oxford: Oxford University Press).

Horsefield, J. Keith (1969) *The International Monetary Fund 1945-1965, Vol. III. Documents* (International Monetary Fund).

JMK XXV, XXVI; Vols XXV and XXVI of *The Collected Writings of John Maynard Keynes*, ed. Donald Moggridge (1980) (London: Macmillan).

Kolm, Serge-Christophe (1970) 'Les États-unis Bénéficient ils du "Droit de Seigneur" '?, *Kyklos*, Fasc. 3, pp. 425-45.

Tobin, James (1984) 'On the Efficiency of the Financial System', *Lloyds Bank Review*, July.

Triffin, Robert (1960) *Gold and the Dollar Crisis* (New Haven, Conn.: Yale University Press).

Williamson, John (1977) *The Failure of World Monetary Reform 1971-74* (London: Nelson).

Williamson, John (1981) Review of JMK XXV, XXVI, *Economic Journal*, June, pp. 541-4.

Williamson, John (1985) 'On the System in Bretton Woods', *American Economic Review*, May, pp. 74-9.

Worswick, David and James Trevithick, (eds) (1983) *Keynes and the Modern World* (Cambridge: Cambridge University Press).

DISCUSSION

Official Discussant, *Mr Graham Bird*: The principal purpose of this brief paper is to consider the question of whether the developing countries would have been better off had the Keynes Plan been adopted at Bretton Woods rather than the less ambitious White Plan.

It is obviously impossible to provide a satisfactory scientific answer to such a hypothetical question, and there must always remain doubts about how the Keynes Plan would have worked in practice. However, in an attempt to provide some insight into the matter, the approach adopted here is to examine the two extreme views. Namely, on the one hand, that adoption of the Keynes Plan would have made no difference; and, on the other, that it would have made a great deal of difference.

From this examination the conclusion emerges that the Plan would, in principle, have provided a superior international environment for developing countries, but that, in practice, many of the features that would have been most attractive to them would probably have been modified in such a way as to reduce their attraction. This conclusion is very similar to the one reached in John Williamson's paper.

BACKGROUND ISSUES

Before moving on to examine the extreme views it is useful to bear in mind the ways in which the international financial system impinges on developing countries.

First, it does this through the general nature of the adjustment mechanism, the nature of reserve assets, and the method of liquidity creation. Developing countries may, for example, lose out under generalised exchange rate flexibility, and from a

107

system based on the dollar, where reserve growth, in significant part, reflects the balance of payments position of the United States rather than the needs of the system for reserves.[1]

Secondly, the specifics of the international financial system will also be important. To what extent are developing countries viewed as constituting a special case within the system, and are special facilities provided to help deal with their particular problems?

Another factor to bear in mind, which leads on from this, is that it is very misleading to look at developing countries as if they form an homogeneous group. They do not. The problems faced by middle and higher income less-developed countries (LDCs) can be very different from those faced by low income countries, and the appropriate policies can therefore also be different. Thus, it is a gross, and often inaccurate, simplification to see aspects of the international financial system as being either in or against the interests of 'developing countries'. Some aspects may be simultaneously in the interests of one sub-group of LDCs and against the interests of another sub-group. A more disaggregated approach is required, and this needs to be remembered in what follows.[2]

EXTREME VIEWS

Let us now return to examine the extreme views mentioned earlier, and begin by looking at the effect on developing countries of the system envisaged in the Keynes Plan.

THE SYSTEM IN GENERAL

As noted earlier one extreme view is that the Keynes Plan would have made no difference to developing countries. Basically, this view regards the nature of the world's financial system – or, indeed, non-system – as a function of more fundamental factors, including structural trends with respect to productivity and income elasticities, and macroeconomic policy. In this context, the international financial system is seen as the dependent variable rather than the independent one. Recent economic history seems to provide at least some casual support for such a viewpoint. It was the stability of economic fundamentals that helped sustain the Bretton Woods system during the 1950s and 1960s and their instability that led to the introduction of floating. The alternative view is that adoption of the Keynes Plan would have made all the difference to developing countries. This view rests on a number of arguments. First, the Plan would have led to more sensible policies relating to the nature of reserve assets and of reserve growth. The international financial system would not have been based on the dollar but on bancor, and many of the problems associated with the key role of the dollar, and indeed other currencies, would therefore have been avoided. Furthermore, reserve growth would have been in line with the growth in the need for reserves as revealed by the growth in world trade.

Secondly, the degree of exchange-rate flexibility envisaged in the Plan would have resulted in the quicker elimination of disequilibria than occured in the latter years of the Bretton Woods system, and would have removed some of the burden of adjustment from demand management policies which otherwise were being asked to achieve both internal and external targets. By contrast, since 1973 the claim might be that the excesses of a flexible rate regime, in terms of volatility and currency misalignment, could have been avoided.

Thirdly, the Keynes Plan strongly emphasises the need for a symmetrical distribution of the adjustment burden between deficit and surplus countries. The theme crops up a number of times in the text of the Plan, for example,

It is. . .necessary. . .to have means of restraining improvident borrowers. But the Clearing Union must also seek to discourage creditor countries from leaving unused large liquid balances which ought to be devoted to some positive purpose.

For excessive credit balances necessarily create excessive debit balances for some other party.

The Plan contains proposals for dealing with this problem by imposing a tax on excessive bancor credits and by encouraging 'discussion' with surplus countries about appropriate policy. Such discussion, aimed at reducing the size of surpluses, could have resulted in a more expansionary world economy.

Fourthly, Keynes viewed as deserving 'the greatest possible emphasis' the scope for using the Clearing Union for international purposes other than those to which it was essentially directed. Thus he argued that, 'the Union might become the pivot of the future economic government of the world'. Under such a system the possibility of pursuing global macroeconomic policy, such as the counter-cyclical use of charges proposed in paragraph 7 of the Provisions of the Plan, or of coordinating macroeconomic policy in different countries, might have been realised. If the view is taken that it is the lack of policy coordination which has caused many of the world's recent economic problems, this feature of the Keynes Plan becomes particularly attractive.

Finally, Keynes noted in his Plan the adverse effects of the instability of primary product prices for the world economy.

> At present a falling off in effective demand in the industrial consuming countries causes a price collapse which means a corresponding break in the level of incomes and of effective demand in the raw material producing centres, with a further adverse reaction, by repercussion, on effective demand in the industrial centres; and so, in the familiar way, the slump proceeds from bad to worse. And when the recovery comes, the rebound to excessive demand through the stimulus of inflated prices promotes, in the same evil manner, the excesses of the boom. (Keynes, 1942)

In the Treasury Memorandum from which the above quotation is taken he developed the idea of a system of buffer stocks or 'commod control' to help reduce such instabilities and suggested that the finance necessary to run such a scheme could come from the Clearing Union. If one subscribes to a Kaldorian explanation of inflation and recession, in the 1970s,[3] which is very much in this Keynesian tradition, then clearly a proposal which would have attacked the root cause of the problem would have had considerable benefit, not only for developing countries but for the world economy as a whole.

The System's Specifics

Looking at the specifics of the international financial system the questions are whether the Keynes Plan would have reduced the needs of developing countries for special action and whether special action would more likely have been undertaken. Before addressing these questions it may be useful to identify some of the factors that might make special action necessary on behalf of developing countries. These include: an adverse and persistent deterioration in their terms of trade; export instability; inadequancy of their international reserves; impaired access to private capital; debt problems; and limited scope for quick adjustment. Let us now present the view that adoption of the Keynes Plan would have made a significant contribution to alleviating these problems.

First, via 'commod control', some influence might have been exerted over developing countries' terms of trade, primarily by reducing the degree of instability about the trend. One structural deficiency of developing countries' balance of payments could therefore have been ameliorated.

Secondly, reserve inadequacy might have been eliminated by the vastly more substantial quantity of reserves that there would have been under the Keynes Plan.[4] In relation to this the impaired access to private capital which would have been more marked under the Plan, incorporating as it did proposals to control the movement of capital, would not have mattered too much. Indeed the greater emphasis on financing deficits through reserve creation rather than through borrowing would have reduced the extent of the debt problem.

Thirdly, the conditionality attached to overdrafts from the Clearing Union might have been more appropriate to the needs of developing countries by placing more emphasis on the exchange rate and less emphasis on credit ceilings. Devaluation is here seen as being more likely to achieve the required structural changes and to accommodate adjustment within a growing economy than are deflationary policies based on tight financial control.

Fourthly, the use of bancor to finance development agencies, as proposed in the Keynes Plan, might have enabled such agencies to make a greater contribution to economic development. With more emphasis on multilateral aid, greater assistance could have been offered to the poorest countries in the world. Keynes argued that:

> where financial contributions are required for some purpose of general advantage, it is a great facility not to have to ask for specific contributions from any named country, but to depend rather on the anonymous and impersonal aid of the system as a whole. We have here a genuine organ of truly international government.

Finally, as the proposals of the Brandt Commission illustrate, reforms directed at encouraging financial flows to developing countries perhaps fit best into a Keynesian framework which emphasises the potential macroeconomic benefits from income redistribution and the implied mutuality of interests.

Now let us turn to the alternative view, namely that the Keynes Plan would have made no contribution towards dealing with the specific problems of developing countries, or, indeed, that it would have made things worse for them. This view is again based on a number of arguments. First, the history of the evolution of the international financial system provides examples where the special interests of developing countries have led to reform. Thus the Compensatory Financing Facility was established in

1963 to help deal with the payments problems caused by exogenuously generated export shortfalls. The facility has been liberalised subsequently on a number of occasions. The Buffer Stock Financing Facility was established in 1969 to assist countries whose involvement with buffer stock schemes created payments problems. The Extended Fund Facility was introduced in 1974 to assist with longer term and more structurally orientated payments difficulties. A Trust Fund and Subsidy Accounts have been used to increase concessionary assistance to the poorest countries. The SDR scheme in its early years incorporated an informal aid link, since the rate of interest on net use was well below the market rate and developing countries were significant net users.

Secondly, commodity stabilisation through buffer stocking arrangements is subject to a number of problems both in principle and in practice. Stabilising price will not always stabilise earnings and may indeed destabilise them; depending on whether the price instability arises from demand side or supply side factors. Furthermore, buffer stock intervention may lead to inappropriate market signals being posted to producers and consumers. In any case, there is the problem of distinguishing between cyclical and secular price changes. There are then the practical problems of storage, and the rather chequered experiences with commodity agreements.[5]

Thirdly, international reserves would simply not have been allowed to expand at the rate implied by the Keynes Plan. The quantity of reserves envisaged there would have resulted in a major inflationary problem and this would not have been to the advantage of developing countries.

Fourthly, even though the emphasis on reserve creation might superficially have averted debt problems, the Keynes Plan would not have dealt adequately with the problem of economic mismanagement in developing countries. Indeed, by increasing significantly the quantity of low conditionality finance the means for encouraging necessary adjustment would have been largely lost.

Finally, and still according to this extreme view, credit ceilings may be seen as the best available macroeconomic performance criterion since data on credit are relatively easily available, credit reflects in general how the economy is performing, and finally it is something over which the government may exert direct control. Of course, if a monetary perspective is adopted, domestic credit creation assumes the principal, if not exclusive, role in explaining the balance of payments.

A BRIEF ASSESSMENT OF THE ISSUES RAISED

Very many of the points raised above are contentious and could be debated at length. Many volumes have been written on topics such as commodity stabilisation and IMF conditionality.[6] Rather than undertaking a full assessment of the issues involved, this section attempts to draw some fairly general conclusions which broadly support those reached in the paper by John Williamson.

In principle, and on balance, it does seem that the Keynes Plan would have offered developing countries a superior international environment both in general and in terms of the specifics of the system. While the nature of the international financial regime is not the only determinant of global macroeconomic performance, and may not even be the most important determinant, it is difficult to believe that it exerts no influence. In any case, the closer coordination of macroeconomic policy and the greater symmetry in adjustment that might have been encouraged had the Keynes Plan been activated would have helped to avoid many of the causes of payments disequilibria. It remains unclear, however, whether implementation of the Keynes Plan and of commod control would have served to avoid all the global macroeconomic problems of the post 1973 period. This requires the acceptance of the Kaldorian thesis and the rejection of alternative explanations, of which there are a number.[7]

On the specifics, developing countries would have had some of the constraints on development removed by the additional reserves implied by the Keynes Plan. There is also some reason to believe that a greater emphasis on low conditionality finance than currently exists would be helpful to developing countries. Where adjustment is necessary, the shift in the balance away from credit ceilings and towards exchange rate policy would also be beneficial, though one needs to recognise that exchange rate changes may have to be accompanied by other policies to encourage a switch of resources into the traded goods sector.[8] It is also true, however, that economic mismanagement is a frequent impediment to development – no matter how well intentioned are the objectives underpinning it – and that the sceptics of buffer stocking arrangements can make a strong case.

In practical terms it seems doubtful whether the failure to adopt the Keynes Plan has been of much significance to developing countries. Even in the system as it has operated they have been able to achieve reforms that have been to their advantage. Moreover, many of the aspects of the Keynes Plan that, in principle, would have been most helpful to them would almost certainly have been modified had the Plan actually been adopted. With little doubt the growth of reserves would not have occurred at the rate envisaged in the Plan. The pressures on surplus countries to adjust would probably have been inadequate, as indeed the 'scarce currency clause' proved to be.

Perhaps the principal lesson for developing countries to learn from the Keynes Plan is that it is very difficult to get apparently radical and far reaching proposals accepted within the international community. At a time when LDCs hanker after a New International Economic Order perhaps they should be examining more fully ways in which relatively minor reforms to existing arrangements could be made to their benefit.

NOTES

All unspecified quotes come from the 'Keynes Plan'; see Grubel (1963).

1. This conceals the question of whether the supply of reserves is demand determined even under a system based on the dollar.

2. For a fuller development of this theme see Bird (1986).
3. Kaldor (1976).
4. See Williamson (this volume) for some calculations of the size of this reserve growth.
5. For a fuller examination of buffer stock schemes see Bird (1982) and Newbery and Stiglitz (1981).
6. On the former see for example Newbery and Stiglitz (1981), on the latter see Williamson (1983) and Killick *et al.* (1984).
7. For a review of these alternative explanations see Bird (1985).
8. For a further development of this theme see Killick, *et al., op cit.*

REFERENCES

Bird, Graham (1982) *The International Monetary System and the Less Developed Countries*, second ed (London: Macmillan).
Bird, Graham (1985) *World Finance and Adjustment: An Agenda for Reform* (London: Macmillan).
Bird, Graham (1986) *International Financial Policy and Economic Development: A Disaggregated Approach* (London: Macmillan).
Grubel, Herbert G. (1963) *World Monetary Reform: Plans and Issues*, Ch. 2, Proposals for an International Clearing Union (Oxford: Oxford University Press).
Kaldor, N. (1976) 'Inflation and Recession in the World Economy', *Economic Journal*, December, pp. 703-14.
Keynes, J.M. (1942) 'The International Control of Raw Materials', Treasury Memorandum, reprinted in *Journal of International Economics*, 4, pp. 299-315.
Killick, T., Bird, G., Sharpley, J., and Sutton, M. (1984) *The Quest for Economic Stabilization: the IMF and the Third World* (London: Heinemann/Overseas Development Institute).
Newbery, David M.G. and Stiglitz, Joseph E. (1981) *The Theory of Commodity Price Stabilization: A Study in the Economics of Risk* (Oxford: Oxford University Press).
Williamson, John (ed.) (1983) *IMF Conditionality* (London: Institute for International Economics).

INTRODUCTION II
M.J.C. *Vile* (Chairman)

We are especially fortunate in having Mr Edward Heath to give the final paper in today's Seminar. The views of any former Prime Minister on the theme of Economic Development would command our interest and respect, but Edward Heath has an expertise and authority which is far more specific and germane. For it is pre-eminently as a leading member of the Independent Commission on Development Issues – the Brandt Commission – whose Report, published in 1980, so focused world attention on the North–South divide that he is to speak to us today. In July, the University took pride in conferring an honorary doctorate on Mr Heath: in two weeks' time he will take part in the Congregation at which Herr Brandt is honoured in like fashion. There is, then, a particular apositeness in now asking Mr Heath to speak on the theme of 'International Keynesianism: The Problem of the North–South Divide'.

INTERNATIONAL KEYNESIANISM:
THE PROBLEM OF THE NORTH-SOUTH DIVIDE
Edward Heath

It is palpably the case that there is a deflationary bias in the international economic order: this has been so for the whole of this decade so far. It must be corrected.

Why palpably? Because there are over 25 *million* men and women unemployed in the OECD alone. The number of unemployed in the rest of the world is not quantified. I think we can accept, in part at least, that uncompetitiveness is the cause of unemployment in Britain. If we are not competitive, there is less demand to buy British goods, not only in export markets, but in our home market too. But uncompetitiveness cannot be the explanation of the high international level of unemployment: for after all – by definition – we cannot *all* be uncompetitive.

The answer is that there is a lack of demand in the international system. People say that international trade is at a record level, and so it is. And this is an indication that demand has grown. But demand cannot be seen in isolation. If employment is to be preserved, demand must keep pace with productivity. For if the demand for goods remains stable and rising productivity means that it takes less labour to produce these goods, naturally unemployment will rise. Demand may have grown, but it has not grown fast enough.

It is difficult to quantify the deficiency in demand. That is an area for detailed economic research. Full global figures are not available, but if we look at the OECD Big Seven for which we have the fullest data and take final expenditure upon the Gross Domestic Product as an indication of demand, graphing it against productivity (defined as output per man hour), we have a rough picture in which since about the end of 1980 or the beginning of 1981 productivity growth has exceeded growth in demand. If we look at the position for the United Kingdom alone, the pattern is similar, though rather more marked. I strongly suspect that the global picture if it could be sketched out would be the same. What then are the causes of insufficiency of demand which is the only plausible explanation of world unemployment and the present fragile position of the international economy? It does not seem that net saving by households is detracting from demand internationally. In the United States, for example, in spite of exorbitant real interest rates, the savings ratio remains relatively low. The answer lies in the incorrect management of the international financial system by private sector institutions, by national governments and through them by the international agencies themselves. This has manifested itself in the inept recycling of the OPEC surpluses by the private sector in the 1970s, the failure of national governments to coordinate their economic policies through the OECD to offset cyclical factors in the 1980s and the debt crisis which they spawned to which no effective solution has yet been agreed.

All these factors are linked, and it benefits us not at all to try to apportion blame. We are all in this mess together and our common purpose must be to get out of it together. How? By a return to the policies of cooperation, coordination and consensus that characterised those successful decades after the Second World War. What I am urging is a return to international demand management. Yet I would stress that it is not, nor has it ever been, my view that demand management alone is sufficient. Demand management is a necessary, but not a sufficient, element of economic policy, whether at national or international level.

I do not accept the Chancellor of the Exchequer's claim made last year in his Mais Lecture that he had effected a reverse in the roles of macro and microeconomic policy. His analysis is a calumny of oversimplification and a gross caricature of those of us who have advocated demand management. We have always know that macroeconomic policy alone would never be sufficient to produce real growth: but if we accept that competitiveness and productivity are also vital factors, it is clear not only that demand must rise alongside productivity gains, but also that the type of supply side reforms that encourage competitiveness are far, far easier to achieve if our managers can invest in the confidence that there will be a market for the extra goods that high productivity will permit them to produce.

Nor have I ever believed that inflation could be controlled by microeconomic policy alone. Money supply and monetary theory were taught as part of Modern Greats even when I was at Balliol! But I am also quite sure that our high unemployment is part of the cost of the failure to use micro as well as macroeconomic tools to control inflation. So the proper roles of macro and micro-policy are far less distinct than the Chancellor would have us believe, and their proper relationship is a complementary one in balanced economic policy.

How are we to implement 'demand management' at an international level? We can treat this question in either the short or the long term. In the long run, we shall have to develop the roles of the World Bank, the International Monetary Fund and the GATT to allow them more adequate resources, structure and power for the purpose. In the short run, we must tackle the key problems in international finance today: the debt crisis, the United States deficit, interest rates, the level of the dollar and the question of who will assume the job of being the locomotive of the world economy when the United States upturn runs out of steam. Let us begin with the debt crisis. It is as good a place to start as any and we shall see that all those key questions are inextricably inter-linked.

The essentials of the debt crisis are that taken together the non-OPEC developing countries owe the developed world an amount of about US$800 billion, and that they are unable to service these debts. Why? This is the result of a combination of factors. Since much of the debt was incurred interest rates have risen sharply (partly as a result of the United States budget deficit), the price of the oil they import has increased dramatically and the price of the commodities they sell to pay for what they buy has fallen. They are thus squeezed from all sides.

What is the consequence of this for us? First, that our banking system and the whole system of international trade on which we depend is placed in jeopardy. Secondly, that the inability of the debtor nations to buy what they need to continue their development means that we in the developed countries are unable to supply them, which we need to do to sustain employment.

It is not that these countries have debts that is important. Industrialising countries almost always have debt: this was true of the United States, Canada and Australia among others during the nineteenth century. It is the ability of the countries to service these debts that is important. For it is upon their abiliy to service debt that their ability to gain new credit to finance new projects rests. And this depends not only upon earning a positive rate of return for individual projects, but also upon access to the required foreign exchange to satisfy repayment obligations. The satisfaction of repayment obligations is crucial to confidence, and it is upon confidence that the system rests. This confidence has broken down and this is the explanation for the most extraordinary reversal in the direction of capital flows.

Bank for International Settlements figures show that in the first quarter of 1985, for the first time since records were kept, there was a decrease of lending to the non-OPEC developing countries. During that period $1.7 billion flowed out of these countries compared with a net inflow of $2.4 billion during the equivalent quarter of 1984.

Mexico's rescheduling in August was billed as a way of paving the road for the resumption of normal borrowing. But this is easier said than done. New voluntary extensions of short-term trade credit has been more than offset by net repayments of existing loans. Banks have curtailed new lending even to developing countries that have avoided debt problems.

Because of their exposure to Third World debt risks, banks are reluctant to increase still further their lending to debtor nations. Any new money has been largely involuntary: the IMF has threatened not to put up money to help debtors service their debts unless the banks accepted the need for new money for new projects to earn rates of return and thus facilitate repayment in the future.

It is now clear that many debtors see that they are being forced to choose between funding their debt service and funding growth. This is a highly dangerous situation. Take Latin America, for example. According to some estimates, the net transfer of capital out of the region averaged $25 billion per annum between 1982 and 1984. This is roughly equivalent to 25 per cent of regional expenditure. The magnitude of the transfer and its implication both for the economies of Latin America and of the developed world have not been fully perceived.

The truth is that it is a major element in introducing a deflationary bias in the international system. According to the figures in the latest Inter-American Development Bank Report, the ratio of investment to GNP declined from 26 per cent in 1981 to 20 per cent in 1983. Similarly, per capita GNP has declined dramatically after 30 years of uninterrupted growth. And this represents a great deal of goods not purchased by *them* and output not produced by *us*.

But where has the money gone? Much of it has fled to Wall Street to finance the burgeoning United States budget deficit. The $200 billion budget deficit, which is mirrored in a trade deficit of $150 billion has caused economic change to the international economic order. It is true that it has administered an immense boost to international demand which has to some extent ameliorated the deflationary bias in the system. But at the same time, the combination of the deficit and the extreme monetarist doctrine of the Federal Reserve Bank has produced exorbitant real interest rates and an over-valued dollar. These factors have acted to re-double the burden upon the debtor nations: it is estimated that for every point increase in interest rates, the annual interest burden on these unfortunate countries increases by between $200 and $400 million.

A large element in the growth of the United States budget deficit has been the arms build-up under President Reagan. The proposed defence budget for 1986 is $313.7 billion, while expenditure in the current year will exceed $284 billion. Yet according to the Mitsubishi Research Institute, infrastructure spending is at least 1.6 times higher in its economic effects than military spending. We have always believed that the multiplier effect of spending was much stronger in third world countries. So the diversion of spending from infrastructure build-up in the Third World to armaments spending in the First can itself be said to introduce a deflationary bias into the international economic order. Equally worrying is that the present United States upturn is unlikely to be sustainable, in the medium let alone the long term. Worse, the trade deficit that is its concomitant is prompting increasing pressure for protection in the United States. We saw the consequences of that in the 1930s.

In the 1985 UNCTAD report it is estimated that one-third of exports from developing countries are affected by some form of protectionism and that 65 per cent of their manufacturing exports are restrained by non-tariff measures. If these barriers were dismantled and the developing world allowed preferential access to industrial markets, their export earnings could be increased by $34 billion annually. The present value of a $34 billion increase in earnings is calculated to be $700 billion, and in other words 85 per cent of Third Word debt.

UNCTAD goes on to assess the impact of the debt crisis upon the OECD. It has estimated that about eight million jobs have been lost in the developed world over the past three years as a result of reduced imports by the major debtors in Africa and Latin America. About 90 per cent of this effect would seem to have fallen on Europe, which has suffered a loss of 6.8 million man years since the debt crisis broke in 1982: more than two million jobs in each year.

What is the prospect that faces us now that the slowdown in the United States economy has begun? Even leaving aside the threat posed by protectionism, we face a difficult situation. Not even the Keynesian Aunt Sally of monetarist demonology would urge the continued application of fiscal stimulus to the United States economy by allowing a continual escalation of the budget deficit. This represents a misallocation of resources on a global scale, for which we will all suffer. In such a situation, the public sector in the United States would continue, because of the vast scale of the United States economy, to pre-empt a lion's share of available international capital, starving more worthwhile prospects and ventures. Diminishing returns have already set in: the accelerator has ceased to respond.

Yet while the rest of the world will continue to be deprived of badly needed capital that it can use to better economic effect, if United States policy remains unchanged, high interest will continue to hit the Third World long after the partial compensation of expanding United States imports of their products has ceased. Already, on the back of slowing United States growth, the economies of the Far East have started to slow. Europe has had only slow growth throughout the present 'recovery' in the international economy.

Now at last, belatedly but nonetheless welcome, governments have begun to realise that this situation must be 'managed'. The Group of Five meeting in New York in September and the IMF meeting at Seoul last month heralded a major change in the balance of opinion about management of the international economy. At the Group of Five, the United States Treasury Secretary on behalf of the Administration explicitly recognised that the dollar was 'over-valued' and that action was necessary to ensure a 'soft landing'. This was a major change in the rhetoric of an administration that had previously recognised no values but those of a market, the omni-competence of which was completely unqualified. It was echoed by our own Treasury.

Even more dramatically, Mr Baker's initiative on Third World debt announced at the IMF Annual Conference in Seoul represents an abrupt volte-face. Belatedly, the Reagan Administration has recognised that deflationary adjustment policies are unlikely to re-establish the credit-worthiness of debtor nations. Having long downplayed the role of the World Bank the United States is now recognising the importance of its proper role in assisting in the implementation of long-term policies.

This is undoubtedly a step in the right direction, even if the $30 billion package is clearly insufficient when compared to the scale of the problem. Three years ago, when we published the second Brandt report, we estimated that at least $85 billion will be required. Since then, there has been improvement in the balance of payments situation of many debtor nations, but at the same time, it is recognised that the resources Mr Baker hopes will be made available will permit only fifteen countries to be included in the proposed scheme. Further, Mr. Baker has conceded that it will be impossible to deal even with all fifteen at once. He wants to start with a 'reasonably major debtor'.

In outline, Mr Baker's plan is a three-part initiative. It recognises that reliance on IMF adjustment or austerity programmes linked to short-term loans, though necessary, are insufficient. (I am glad that the Reagan Administration has realised this: it was of course the reason why the World Bank was created in the first place.) Thus, alongside 'a continued central role' for the IMF, Baker attaches new priority to a second element, the World Bank and other multilateral development banks in supporting the debtors in pursuit of 'market-oriented policies for growth'. Thirdly, he proposes increased lending by private banks in support of comprehensive economic adjustment, as guided by the IMF and the World Bank.

The aim is to promote economic growth now that many of them have carried out more or less successful external adjustments. As well as continuing with IMF-type fiscal, monetary and exchange rate policies, they would be expected to adopt 'supply-side' policies of a type long advocated by the World Bank. These include liberalisation of foreign trade, inward direct investment, reform of tax and public expenditure arrangements and moves towards a rational structure of relative prices by withdrawing subsidies and ending controls.

Mr Baker has suggested that the commercial banks should advance an extra $20 billion over the next three years to support supply-sided strengthening measures. In return he advocated an increase of 50 per cent in lending by the multilateral development banks, from the expected level of $6 billion in each of the next three years to $9 billion. Since there are to be about $2 billion a year repayments, the net increase in credit outstanding, would be about $20 billion over the 3 years, (or about $10 billion more than had been expected). This represents an annual increase of about 17 per cent a year on the $34 billion of multilateral development banks' credit outstanding to the 15 'Baker countries'.

Nevertheless, the $20 billion in new money from the commercial banks would represent an annual growth in loans of only 2.5 per cent in each of the next three years. This is, of course, negative in real terms, and is certainly slower than the rate at which banks generally expect to increase their capital. Even so, it does represent an improvement on the present situation in which lending is shrinking in nominal as well as real terms.

Thus, the exposure of commercial banks will decline, while the exposure of the World Bank will rise by 50 per cent. At the same time, the exposure of the IMF is likely to remain roughly steady at $15 billion: it is just about at the limit of its resources. Our hope must be that this will allow the World Bank and the IMF to exercise greater leadership, notably through cofinancing of loans, which in the medium term will restore confidence and therefore allow a resumption of new capital transfer to the developing world by the private sector.

My own feeling is that much greater resources will be required by the World Bank and the IMF to enable them to carry out the role of restoring confidence to the extent where the Third World's requirements of funds for adjustment and investment can be met. Mr Baker's plan does have one striking political advantage, however. It is that a general capital increase to finance the higher rate of activity of the World Bank can probably be put off until 1987. This means that it need not go before Congress (and other national legislatures) until after the November 1986 mid-term election. In a sense, therefore, we are still paying the price of Poujardist sentiments about international economic management. The Reagan Administration has begun to recognise the direction in which it must go, but is held back by the spirit in Congress, which it, itself, did so much to foster.

What is needed is reserves on a sufficient scale for both the IMF and the World Bank to enable them to get properly to grips with the debt crisis. Rather than just fighting fires and nudging countries back when they get too close to the brink, we could begin to construct a long-term solution. And the sooner we do that, the sooner we will be able to put our own people back to work in the developed countries.

The World Bank should be given a substantial capital injection as soon as possible to finance not only structural and sectoral adjustment loans, but also project loans. Equally, the IMF now almost at the limit of its resources, has no spare capacity to permit it to deal with the balance of payments consequence of a world trade downturn in the developed countries. It seems likely that its role in the foreseeable future will be little more than rolling-over existing credits: this will give it substantially less economic influence and leverage than if it had the resources to assist.

Finally, alongside a further increase in IMF capital, I would welcome a new issue of Special Drawing Rights. There has been none such since 1981, and the time has come to give a boost to world liquidity and demand. This would have the effect of relieving upward pressure on interest rates. I can already hear the cries of 'inflation, inflation', but this is to misunderstand. Such an increase would not be inflationary in present economic conditions (though I recognise that there are circumstances where it would be). It would be counter-deflationary, not inflationary. It would play some part in offsetting the deflationary bias in the present international order.

It seems that, at best, the two-pronged Baker initiative through the Group of Five and at Seoul will keep the world economy afloat. The scale of the proposals is insufficient to boost the world into a new phase of growth.

Since the Group of Five meeting, central bank intervention to engineer a sustained but orderly decline in the value of the dollar has scarcely materialised. While I believe strongly that the central banks have a role in smoothing currency movements, I do not think that they can override market forces. In the end it will only be a reduction in United States interest rates, partly the result of the deficit, but also the product of monetary extremism at the

Fed. that will allow an orderly reduction in the dollar rate. Otherwise, we can expect the dollar to continue to ride high, until there is a change – most likely an abrupt one – in market sentiment, leading to the feared 'hard landing'. This will happen when the markets realise – as they realised in the 1970s in the wake of Vietnam – that even the United States cannot sustain endless borrowing. So, however much I welcome the signs from the Group of Five that cooperative management of currencies is to be resumed, I regret that without an agreement by the United States government to cut its interest rates and begin to reduce its new borrowings, this will be largely ineffective in promoting greater exchange rate stability and an orderly reduction in the value of the dollar.

A reduction in interest rates would of itself provide some stimulation to the international economy. It would relieve pressures in the Third World, fostering investment there as well as in the industrialised countries. But the counter-part of the Group of Five decision to resume economic cooperation in currency management must be a wider agreement within the OECD to renew greater coordination of fiscal and monetary policies. The aim of this exercise must be to avoid a new recession in the world economy as United States growth slows, bringing with it the risk of a slump precipitated by sharp deterioration of the debt situation with all its concomitant risks for the banks.

At long last, pressure is now mounting for a convergence of economic policy in the leading industrial nations. Perhaps coordination would be a better term than convergence, since the prescriptions advocated are not identical in the case of each economy. Germany and Japan, for example, are urged to relax their emphasis on tight fiscal and monetary policy and to become more expansionary. At the same time, the United States should pursue a much tighter fiscal policy, perhaps coupled with a slightly looser monetary regime. This is the first time since 1978 that the body of opinion has shifted behind a coordinated approach to world economic management. The long 'U' turn is now almost complete.

Few people any longer put faith in 'supply side' means *alone* to reduce unemployment. There is still dispute about whether United States superior economic growth in 1983–84 was due to the enormous fiscal stimulation of the budget deficit or to supply side flexibility. No doubt the robustness of the supply side was important and we in Britain must put every effort into the strength of our industry and commerce, but the emerging consensus puts emphasis on the crucial part played by the fiscal stimulus in circumstances when the supply side was in a strong position to respond to the challenge of a boost to demand by raising output rather than prices.

Of course, inflation will be the charge levelled against me by the monetarists and the neo-classicists. These fears are misconceived and rest on misunderstanding of the nature and causes of inflation. In particular, a misreading of the French experience of 1983–84. In France it was not reflation *per se* that caused inflation, but the way in which reflation there was achieved (direct increases in industry's costs) and the context in which it was carried out, against the background of contraction by her principal trading partners.

Why has not the much stronger United States reflation led to inflation? The answer is firstly because it did not increase costs and secondly because the reflation in the United States was not accompanied by fiscal stimulus in the rest of the OECD, which would put pressure on raw material prices. It was a bottleneck in the supply of raw materials – especially, but, of course, not only the 'political bottleneck' of the OPEC cartel in the case of oil – that caused the inflation of the 1970s. Which brings us back to the debt crisis: for there is another risk in the massive reduction in investment in the Third World. Unless we get the investment in the extraction of commodities, the risk of renewed inflation as we get a proper international recovery will be increased. The bottleneck in supply of raw materials may, as a result of neglect, be far worse than we experienced in the early part of the last decade. So, here too, in our own interests, we must look to a solution of the debt crisis.

DISCUSSION

Official Discussant, Dr I.M.D. Little: I was invited to be a discussant of Mr Heath's paper, but the paper was not disclosed. On the day, Mr Heath gave an entertaining, forceful and wide-ranging speech: but it moved too fast and was too wide-ranging for me to be able to come up with an instant and cogent commentary.

Knowing Mr Heath's adherence to the views of the Brandt Commission, of which he was a member, I had decided to take up a central issue raised by the Brandt report – that of 'massive transfers' (p. 67 ff. and p. 241 ff.). A theme of the Brandt Report was 'mutual interest' (p. 64 ff.), and it was maintained that massive transfers (part increased aid, i.e. concessionary flows, and part loans at commercial rates), would benefit the North as well as the South. The supporting argument was essentially Keynesian. With massive transfers the South would act as a locomotive and pull the North out of its state of under-employment.

This is a beguiling argument for the altruistic. There is no doubt about the great need of the South, nor about unused resources in the North. But it can appeal to the self-interest of the North, only if both (a) a demand-led expansion is good policy for the North, and (b) there is no better way for the North to take up the slack in their economies than by an expansion of Southern demand induced by such massive transfers.

Northern countries can engineer increases in demand without any special measures to increase the flow of funds to the South. A key question is why they have not always done so when resources were underemployed.

A possible reason is that no single country can expand alone for balance-of-payments reasons, while macroeconomic policies are not sufficiently coordinated to ensure that all or most countries expand together. There has been much comment along these lines, with calls for surplus countries, especially Germany and Japan, to act as locomotives (they needed no transfers).

I do not think that the above 'prisoner's dilemma' kind of argument is the heart of the problem. It obviously does not apply to the surplus countries, which have not wanted to expand as much as others might like, for fear of inflation. Moreover, I believe that even the deficit countries of the North (and not only the United States) could go it alone if they did not fear inflation.

There was no difficulty about borrowing in the period 1974–82 as the 'newly-industrialising' countries found. European countries with weak balance-of-payments positions could even now borrow to cover the temporary deficits which expansion would cause. If wage inflation were not ready to burst into flames a fall in the exchange rate would quite soon rectify any deficit so long as there was excess capacity.

So inflation is the heart of the matter. It has been the fear of inflation that has damped expansion, especially in Europe. Without it, the North could have expanded without massive transfers to the South. On both counts, massive transfers were not in the economic interest of the North.

It can be argued that increased demand coming from abroad is less inflationary than a rise in domestic demand, and the cries for a locomotive bear witness that this was indeed believed. The idea is that the terms of trade would be better than if one country, say the United Kingdom, went it alone. This is, however, very uncertain, for a general boom, as in the early 1970s, may well result in worse terms of trade for, say, the United Kingdom, than if it expanded alone in a relatively stagflationary world.

Furthermore, massive transfers, even if they are grants or nearly so, may not much benefit the South. Many countries in the South *did* get massive transfers between 1973 and 1982. In the case of the oil exporters, very large new revenues suddenly accrued to their governments – the equivalent of grants without strings. Other countries such as Brazil, Argentina, and South Korea, borrowed very heavily at real interest rates that were roughly zero until 1979. Some of those who benefited from large new revenues unwisely borrowed heavily as well, e.g. Mexico, Venezuela, and Nigeria. With a few exceptions, the results were disastrous. Many LDC governments had been operating very bad, even unviable, policies. Reform was postponed, and bad policies encouraged. There was appalling waste in the form of hasty ill-chosen industrial and infrastructural investments. Even such an erstwhile paragon of economic virtue as South Korea went off the rails.

The price mechanism is very severely distorted in most LDCs mainly because of bad policies. The yield of an investment calculated at such distorted prices is little or no guide as to whether it will benefit the country, and in particular whether it will raise or reduce the ability of the country to service any debt incurred. But many LDC governments anyway show little concern for the yield of an investment at any set of prices. They are more interested in modern capital-intensive monuments, and other paraphernalia of a modern state that may benefit and gladden the hearts of technocrats, bureaucrats, and politicians, but which do not help and may well indirectly harm the common people.

It is true that events in the 1980s became worse than it was reasonable to expect in the 1970s – with the rise in interest rates, the recession, and the fall in commodity prices. On this account, the returns (often negative) to some investments were worse than it was reasonable to expect. But even if external events had been up to reasonable expectations, the South would have littered many white elephants.

It has not been only bad investment. Cheap capital inflows magnified consumption rises, both private and governmental, in countries that were already benefiting from the oil price rises. Military expenditure also rose rapidly, and the incidence of warfare increased.

The lesson of the past fifteen years is that policies in many Southern countries are not such as to make the receipt of large unsupervised transfers to governments, whether concessionary (i.e. aid) or on commercial terms, advantageous either to lenders or donors) or to the people of the recipient country. I am in favour of such transfers, including aid. But they must be tied to good projects, or be conditional on sound economic policies. The Commercial Banks indulged in massive sovereign lending in the 1970s without regard for what the money was used for, whether it would generate returns to service the debt, and without even knowing how much the borrower already owed. This was much praised at the time, but the results have shown that conditionality, however much disliked by Southern governments and their well-wishers, has to be the order of the future. How large, how massive, transfers can be depends on the willingness of Southern governments to initiate reforms.

I believe the Brandt Commission tried to find mutual interest where it does not exist. In so doing it tended to under-emphasise the role of trade, where long-run benefits for the vast majority of people in the North and the South are most demonstrable. It is remarkable, for instance, that the only mention of the EEC's Common Agricultural Policy in the Report was in a favourable context. Increased protectionism in the North is particularly inappropriate in this stagflationist era. Cheap consumption-good imports, including food, would moderate cost-of-living increases and hence should moderate wage demands. This would raise the overall level of employment which governments can tolerate, given their inflationary fears.

Mr Heath: I think there is a difference of philosophy as well as an economic approach between us. I can understand those who criticise everything which happens in the developing world. I don't share all those criticisms. Of course, there are countries which like to go for status symbols, but then practically every country in the North goes for status symbols. You can say it's done for political reasons or social reasons, and not for purely economic reasons; yes, it is, and this is part of the facts of life, that if politicians are going to survive they have to do some things for political reasons, and if they were just economic analysts then they would remain in universities or colleges. So, when we are dealing with these problems we have to face the facts of life.

I don't use the word 'aid', I loathe the word 'aid', and so does the developing world. The developing world says 'We don't want charity, we want to have a fair opportunity to compete in the world as a whole. We want to be part of the world trade and investment system.' It is investment that is important not charity. We British were the first to realise this. We were first in the Industrial Revolution. We produced all these new industrial goods, and the developing world, which then included the whole of North and South America and a large part of Europe as well as Australasia, said 'We want these things'. And we said 'We will make them for you'. And they said 'Well, we haven't got much money because all we do is sell you raw materials and you don't pay us very much for them'. We said 'Well, you don't have to worry about that. The City of London will look after that'. And by 1914 there was hardly a country in the world whose name was not on the bonds of the City of London: the Czar's empire, France, the United States, Canada, Australia, New Zealand, all the Latin American countries, and we made a good profit out of it. And when we had done that we didn't put the profit into gold bars and put them in the cellar and go and look at them with a candle every week to see if they were still there, we invested it further in more production and more goods, and that's what gave us our economic strength and industrial base which has now been so catastrophically eroded in the last few years. So, I think Dr Little and I have a complete difference of approach in these matters. I accept that sometimes things go wrong, of course they go wrong, but if investments and capital projects are looked after efficiently by an international organisation, with government cooperation, or by some form of private enterprise, governments can do a great deal to see that corruption is excluded and that capital is wisely used.

I also see things from the political side. I still have on my conscience that Dr Busia came to see me when he was Prime Minister of Ghana and he said 'I have an election in six months. If you can give me the money to help provide clean water in each village in Ghana I can win the election and keep democracy.' I couldn't persuade the Chancellor of the Exchequer to provide the money for water in Ghana (I think probably Terence Higgins was responsible for the fact I didn't get it!). And so I had to say to him 'We haven't got the money', and he went back empty handed. He didn't have an election within six months. Before that could take place there was a coup and democracy went from Ghana, and that's been the situation ever since. And so I do look at these matters also from a political point of view because I regard it as necessary to do everything possible to maintain those political systems which are sympathetic to us. I don't take the view that if countries are not sympathetic we should do nothing, because I think it is much better to try and influence them by what we do than to say 'No, we wont't have anything to do with you because we don't like aspects of your system'. But this is the political aspect and that's why I gave a rather broader talk than purely one of economic analysis.

GENERAL DISCUSSION

Mr S. Brickell: May I take up a point made by two of the speakers. Both Mr Heath and Professor Reddaway appear to have suggested that what is required in the world today are men of practical rather than theoretical bent, particularly in regard to the under-developed nations of the world. The implication of their remarks appeared to me to be that theory is all very well but it cannot be applied in the conditions which prevail today in the Third World. The corollary of this view is that the work of Keynes, particularly the *General Theory*, is not applicable. In fact Keynes was a very pragmatic theorist.

Keynes recognised in his major work that the world was always tending to approach a point where it would have all the 'real' assets (production, plant, etc.) that it could employ profitably in the given conditions of income, its distribution, and the consequential propensity to consume. As the real asset stock available to the world economy approaches a level where the marginal return becomes negligible, those wanting to go on accumulating capital will have nowhere to put their money yielding any kind of security or return.

But, of course, as well as real assets, we have 'financial' assets. If the world is providing more savings out of income than can be given a real asset form (such as ships, steel plants, etc.) then these 'surplus savings' must be invested as 'financial assets'). Thus, if the accumulation of capital is to continue (beyond the point where it can be matched by a corresponding accumulation or growing stock of production plant) then we must not forget that the 'financial asset' accumulation must be counter-balanced by an accumulation of 'financial liabilities', that is to say, a growing debt mountain. Yet everyone speaks of debt, debt accumulations and the growth of the world debt as something naughty, as a bad thing, as something that must be prevented.

But you cannot continue to accumulate capital if you are not prepared to countenance a corresponding accumulation of debt. The one is implicit in the other. In essence, the problem facing the world today is that we are trying to accumulate capital while at the same time we are attempting to limit the growth of the 'World Debt Burden'. This is theoretically, practically and logically impossible.

Dr Williamson was on the right lines when he said that the issue of SDR's (or Bancor as it would have been if Keynes had had his way) should be expanded as necessary to meet the demand of savers for financial assets to hold as accumulations of wealth. In this event all those people with incomes greatly in excess of their consumption needs could 'invest' their surpluses in IMF debt (via their own national banking and central bank system perhaps). The IMF, together with other international institutions, would then put the world's annual surpluses at the disposal of the Third World. By this means the aggregate world income, derived from the production of the 'World Product', would be recycled as aggregate demand for that world product, so that demand would always equal supply on world markets without glut, unemployment and Third World starvation. Only in this way can the rich continue to accumulate capital.

Dr Williamson: Just one brief comment: it is not true that you cannot have real investment without increasing debt. Apart from self-financed investment, there is the very important category of finance, which is relatively neglected, and particularly by developing countries in recent years, and that is various forms of equity finance. I am not thinking of direct investment. I can understand why many developing countries may have reservations about accepting large quantities of direct investment. But investment in equities quoted on local stock exchanges in developing countries is very desirable and spreads the risks to the financial markets of the North which are capable of holding it.

Mr Heath: I am sympathetic to some of the points Mr Brickell raises. The problem now is that we have got a situation in which the developing countries have an enormous debt of US$800 billion, and those who made the loans have lost confidence in the ability of the countries to repay, with the result that they are not investing further in those countries. There was a dramatic change in the first quarter of this year because for the first time since 1945 the flow was not into the developing world but out of the developing world to the 'North'. Whereas in the first quarter of 1984 the flow was $2.4 billion from the developed rich countries to the poor; in the first quarter of this year the flow was $1.7 billion from the developing countries back to the rich. Now, this cannot be justified on any moral grounds, nor, I believe, on economic grounds, because it is simply leading to deflationary bias in the whole world economy which we want to avoid. Some say this doesn't matter; it will enable the banks to carry out investment elsewhere. But the fact is that the banks are not doing this because they are over-reacting against the problems of the second half of the 1970s and the beginning of the 1980s as a result of the investment which took place then and the problems to which it has given rise. So, we've got a psychological barrier there at the moment. But so long as the flow is counter to what it has been ever since 1945, then I believe that we are bound to get into deeper and deeper trouble.

Professor Hession: I would like to question Dr Williamson about free trade. The British were so successful in teaching the doctrine of free trade, John Maynard Keynes included, that when the Second World War ended people such as Cordell Hull, the United States Secretary of State, and others, and also the large corporations, believed they had to implement the doctrine of free trade. To talk of Bancor as a feasible monetary policy at that time seemed almost Utopian from a United States point of view, at least for those who were in a position to control monetary and commercial policy.

Dr Williamson: Keynes regarded his monetary system, or something like it, as essential condition to permit free trade to be an acceptable policy to the United Kingdom. He was very ambivalent about free trade throughout his career. He had started off in the 1920s as an enthusiastic free trader, and then he periodically went to the other extreme in some of his statements. But in 1944 he was willing to give it a try because he thought it would have great advantages provided there were enough safeguards, and in particular a monetary system that would make it possible, and he believed that his Clearing Union was what was needed for that purpose, so that from his point of view the two were complements.

Professor Hession: Just so that we reach some understanding: I understood you to say that the Keynes Plan did involve the control of capital movements, and I don't see how you can reconcile controlled capital movements with free trade. I mean, if we take the term in its broadest sense it includes capital as well as commodities.

Dr Williamson: Well, obviously you can define trade, if you want, to include trade in securities, but you don't have to define it that way and that's not the way it has been defined by the GATT; and Keynes's proposal for an International Trading Organisation, of which the GATT was all that emerged in the end, envisaged free trade in goods (not even most services) with a monetary system which would control capital movements, and that is a logical combination.

Mr Heath: If I understood you correctly you said that the British had been so successful in free trade.

Professor Hession: No, in convincing a very large part of the American world (particularly the economics profession) of the validity of the *doctrine* of free trade.

Mr Heath: We have convinced them of the doctrine of free trade? Yes, the Americans have always believed in free trade by other people, and that is still the situation today. They support their farmers and the level of tariffs is far higher than the European

Economic Community. But what I want to add is that our trouble from 1932 onwards was that the United Kingdom was protectionist, and it is from this that many of our evils spring today because our industrialists thought that because the whole of the colonies were in the protective system they could just go on selling the same machinery as they were producing at the end of the nineteenth century to the colonies, and there was no need to do anything else, and that's how we lost a lot of our industrial momentum. The British suffered from protectionism not free trade.

Dr Williamson: I would just like to add one point. I don't want to join in the game of saying that one block of countries is more protectionist than another. Among the three major powers: the United States, the European Community and Japan, I don't think there is very much in it; nothing that one can measure suggests that. But the fact that all three of them trade freely in relative terms compared with the pre-war years, is surely the most important single positive factor behind the international development that we have had in the post-war world. It is this which has given rise to the possibility of export-led growth which is basically what has generalised economic growth around the world, and historically it is quite unprecedented.

Dr Ambrosi: From Mr Heath's vivid (oral) description of General Marshall's political courage in advancing the idea of a European Recovery Program there might arise the question: what has all this to do with Keynes? Indeed Dr Little did voice exactly this question, insisting that we are here at a Keynes seminar and that Keynes himself had very little to say about financial assistance in the sense of the Marshall Plan. But if we look at the finishing passages of Keynes' brilliant and once widely read assessment of *The Economic Consequences of the Peace*, then we find that having the devastations of the First World War before his eyes, Keynes published an extremely eloquent advocacy of an international loan very similar to the one of the European Recovery Program. He was well aware of the almost utopian character of such a scheme at the time of his writing about it and so he did not elaborate it very much. But Keynes was convinced that through a generous peace-time loan by the United States and through the financial assistance of a guarantee fund 'Europe might be equipped with the minimum amount of liquid resources necessary to revive her hopes, to renew her economic organization, and to enable her great intrinsic wealth to function for the benefit of her workers.' It is difficult to judge how far Keynes' analysis of the aftermath of the First World War was to influence General Marshall's bold commitment to financial assistance for Europe after the Second World War. Maybe the Marshall Plan is a case in point for the Keynesian dictum that practical men, 'who believe themselves to be quite exempt from any intellectual influences, are usually the slaves of some defunct economist', (*General Theory*, p. 383). In any case, a Keynes seminar seems to be a very appropriate forum for a plea to have a new Marshall Plan – but now not in order to revive the hopes of Europe but those of the developing countries.

Professor W. Carr: Mr Heath seems to me to be exaggerating the role of will power in history when he credits General George Marshall with a successful personal initiative in June 1947 without the prior knowledge of either the President or the Secretary of State. Already on 8 May, at Cleveland, Dean Acheson spoke with Truman's approval of the need for Congress to appropriate funds to help European recovery (*Plain Speaking: An Oral Biography of Harry S. Truman*, by Merle Miller, New York: Berkley, 1984, p. 258). Marshall, according to Truman, did not know exactly what to say at Harvard. Truman came to the rescue telling him to spell out the details of the plans being worked out in the State Department for aid to Europe. He added to Marshall's embarrassment that this would be called the 'Marshall Plan' (op. cit., p. 262). The fact is that in the summer of 1947 the administration believed as fervently as ever that the old multilateral trading pattern should be restored as quickly as possible. Furthermore, unless the Europeans were given credits they would not be able to buy American food and raw materials.

Above all, fear of communism sweeping through Europe gave a sense of desperate urgency to the actions of the Truman administration. Thus, as so often in international relations, what one individual was saying happened to coincide with the broad thrust of the United States' post-war foreign trade policy.

I gather from Dr Little's comments that self-interest does not oblige the North to effect capital transfers to the South. If so, this will make it immensely more difficult to bring about the change which all liberal minded people regard as a moral imperative. If the North feared the spread of communism in the South as much as the United States did in Europe in the 1940s, this would no doubt introduce the necessary element of self-interest. Failing that, it looks as if our only hope is to re-double our efforts in a great moral crusade against the odds to move people to make sacrifices for the good of others. Whether this will succeed or not does depend in the last resort upon the ability of another great moral crusade – that against nuclear weapons – to prevent the North blowing itself to pieces in the meantime.

Stephen Frowen: In his paper Edward Heath quite rightly stressed the vital importance of strengthening the central role of the International Monetary Fund. He also points out the present inadequacy of IMF resources, as a result of which the IMF can neither play a decisive part in solving the international debt crisis nor deal effectively with the balance of payments consequence of a world trade downturn in the developed countries. Without increased resources the Fund's economic influence and leverage are likely to be considerably smaller than the role Keynes himself envisaged for the IMF in the world economy.

Among ways of raising IMF resources, Mr Heath emphasises – apart from further allocations of Special Drawing Rights – the desirability of increasing IMF capital. However, he does not specify the means by which this goal is to be achieved.

Considering the extent of the underlying problems and the magnitude of the funds required to solve, or at least alleviate, them, a mere further increase in IMF quotas of a size which may be acceptable to the governments of the industrial countries among IMF members, even if accompanied by a further expansion of other existing devices, would scarcely suffice. However, what would enable the IMF to raise funds adequate to cover any required balance of payments financing and to deal more effectively with the international debt crisis would be access to the world's private money and capital markets. But this is just the point on which IMF members cannot agree. In fact, the attitude of some of the leading OECD countries was well expressed by the President of the Deutsche Bundesbank, Karl Otto Pohl, in the following reply to my intervention at a recent conference. In commenting on my plea for IMF access to private capital markets, Mr Pohl said:

> The Bundesbank has always rejected this possibility. A valid reason for me was that I do not believe that this would be in the interest of developing countries because it would probably have the effect that the banks would withdraw from financing developing countries and on balance they would receive fewer credits. However, the main reason is, of course, that one has to be aware that a credit granted by the IMF, and which the IMF has previously refinanced on euromarkets, must in principle be guaranteed by somebody. This would in effect amount to a transfer of risks from the commercial banks to the official sector, i.e. in the case of West Germany the Bundesbank. The willingness of Governments to accept these risks is virtually non-existent. If the IMF did raise funds in private capital markets, this would also substantially reduce the willingness to increase the capital of the IMF, i.e. quotas. In the US such a willingness is anyhow precariously thin. This we experienced in November 1983 when the ratification by Congress of an increase in the IMF quota of the US could only be achieved with great difficulties. Altogether I would not recommend to pursue the idea of the IMF refinancing itself on the world's private capital markets.[1]

Indeed, if this is the official view not only of West Germany but also of other leading industrial countries, then there is regrettably little hope that the IMF will be able to raise the resources required to play the role Mr Heath has in mind for the IMF, i.e. to be one of the corner stones of any solution to the problem of the North–South Divide. The losers of inadequate IMF resources will be the Third World rather than the industrialised economies, for borrowers in developed countries will quite obviously continue to enjoy easy access to private money and capital markets. Evidence of this is the rapidly increasing funds raised by OECD countries, especially in the international bond, floating rate note and Euronote markets, at a time when syndicated Eurocredits – on which many of the developing countries still depend – are marked by a sharp decline.

NOTE

1.   See Besters, H. (ed.) (1984) *Wahrungspolitik auf dem Prufstand*. Symposia of the List Society, New series, Vol. 9 (Baden-Baden: Nomos Verlagsgesellschaft) pp. 138–41 and 151–52.

Sir Austin Robinson: I wonder whether I might suggest another way in which Keynes had an indirect but important influence on the development of a number of the more backward countries of the world?

At the beginning of the war, as everyone will remember, Keynes published his pamphlet 'How to Pay for the War'. I had heard him give this as a lecture in Cambridge. It was obvious that the proper management of a war economy necessitated the regular preparation of a national income estimate. I reported this to Francis Hemming, my boss in the small group of economists then late in 1939 working in the Cabinet Office. He took me to explain it to Sir Edward Bridges, Secretary of the Cabinet, and we were given authority to recruit two persons to tackle the work. We invited James Meade and Richard Stone.

What is relevant to what we then called Colonial Development (it all happened when colonies still existed) came at the next stage, when James Meade had already developed the three approach system. At that time there were hardly any statistics for a colonial territory. I had worked with Lord Hailey on the economic chapters of his vast African Survey. There were very uncertain population guesses, inaccurate foreign trade statistics, in some cases estimates of output of some of the bigger mining countries. There was virtually nothing else. I talked to Richard Stone about the possibility that, by adopting the three-way approach, one might possibly be able to check the guesses that one would have to make of some of the elements and arrive at the order of magnitude of the national income of some of these territories.

With the help of Feodora Stone, then Secretary of the National Institute, we decided to try. We were lucky enough to recruit Phyllis Deane[1] to do the work. We started with Northern Rhodesia (now Zambia) where I had done enough work in the field to be able to help to make guesses. We added Jamaica because we had got Arthur Lewis, himself a Jamaican, to help us. We later added Nyasaland.

When Phyllis Deane had made some progress and it was clear that there were possibilities in this, we let a small economic committee in the Colonial Office, on which I sat under the chairmanship of Arnold Plant, know about it. Sydney Caine[2] and Andrew Cohen,[3] both then on the staff of the Colonial Office became very interested. Andrew Cohen sent out instructions, encouragements, or whatever was appropriate, to the various colonial territories to try to prepare national income estimates, and Phyllis Deane moved over to the Colonial Office. Through the 1950s, many of them called in an expert from this country to make a national income estimate. Without them, serious economic development policies could never have been shaped.

But what I want to say is that all of this had its origins in the system of policy formulation first developed by Keynes in his 'How to Pay for the War'.

NOTES

1. Now Professor Phyllis Deane, FBA, lately President of the Royal Economic society.
2. Subsequently Sir Sydney Caine, Vice-Chancellor of the University of Hongkong and Principal of the London School of Economics.
3. Subsequently Sir Andrew Cohen, last British Governor of Uganda and British representative at the United Nations.

Appendix: The Keynes Plan

PROPOSALS FOR
AN INTERNATIONAL
CLEARING UNION
(Cmd 6437, April 1943)

PREFACE

Immediately after the war all countries who have been engaged will be concerned with the pressure of relief and urgent reconstruction. The transition out of this into the normal world of the future cannot be wisely effected unless we know into what we are moving. It is therefore not too soon to consider what is to come after. In the field of national activity occupied by production, trade and finance, both the nature of the problem and the experience of the period between the wars suggest four main lines of approach:

1. The mechanism of currency and exchange;

2. The framework of a commercial policy regulating the conditions for the exchange of goods, tariffs, preferences, subsidies, import regulations and the like;

3. The orderly conduct of production, distribution and price of primary products so as to protect both producers and consumers from the loss and risk for which the extravagant fluctuations of market conditions have been responsible in recent times.

4. Investment aid, both medium and long term, for the countries whose economic development needs assistance from outside.

If the principles of these measures and the form of the institutions to give effect to them can be settled in advance, in order that they may be in operation when the need arises, it is possible that taken together they may help the world to control the ebb and flow of the tides of economic activity which have, in the past, destroyed security of livelihood and endangered international peace.

All these matters will need to be handled in due course. The proposal that follows relates only to the mechanism of currency and exchange in international trading. It appears on the whole convenient to give it priority, because some general conclusions have to be reached under this head before much progress can be made with the other topics.

In preparing these proposals care has been taken to regard certain conditions, which the groundwork of an international economic system to be set up after the war should satisfy, if it is to prove durable:

(i) There should be the least possible interference with internal national policies, and the plan should not wander from the international *terrain*. Since such policies may have important repercussions on international relations, they cannot be left out of account. Nevertheless in the realm of internal policy the authority of the Governing Board of the proposed Institution should be limited to recommendations, or at the most to imposing conditions for the more extended enjoyment of the facilities which the Institution offers.

(ii) The technique of the plan must be capable of application, irrespective of the type and principle of government and economic policy existing in the prospective member States.

(iii) The management of the Institution must be genuinely international without preponderant power of veto or enforcement to any country or group; and the rights and privileges of the smaller countries must be safeguarded.

(iv) Some qualification of the right to act at pleasure is required by any agreement or treaty between nations. But in order that such arrangements may be fully voluntary so long as they last and terminable when they have become irksome, provision must be made for voiding the obligation at due notice. If many member States were to take advantage of this, the plan would have broken down. But if they are free to escape from its provisions if necessary they may be the more willing to go on accepting them.

(v) The plan must operate not only to the general advantage but also to the individual advantage of each of the participants, and must not require a special economic or financial sacrifice from certain countries. No participant must be asked to do or offer anything which is not to his own true long-term interest.

It must be emphasised that it is not for the Clearing Union to assume the burden of long-term lending which is the proper task of some other institution. It is also necessary for it to have means of restraining improvident borrowers. But the Clearing Union must also seek to discourage creditor countries from leaving unused large liquid balances which ought to be devoted to some positive purpose. For excessive credit balances necessarily create excessive debit balances for some other party. In recognising that the creditor as well as the debtor may be responsible for a want of balance, the proposed institution would be breaking new ground.

THE OBJECTS OF THE PLAN

1. About the primary objects of an improved system of International Currency there is, today, a wide measure of agreement:

(a) We need an instrument of international currency having general acceptability between nations, so that blocked balances and bilateral clearings are unnecessary; that is to say, an instrument of currency used by each nation in its transactions with other nations, operating through whatever national organ, such as a Treasury or a Central Bank, is most appropriate, private individuals, businesses and banks other than Central Banks, each continuing to use their own national currency as heretofore.

(b) We need an orderly and agreed method of determining the relative exchange values of national currency units, so that unilateral action and competitive exchange depreciations are prevented.

(c) We need a *quantum* of international currency, which is neither determined in an unpredictable and irrelevant manner as, for example, by the technical progress of the gold industry, nor subject to large variations depending on the gold reserve policies of individual countries; but is governed by the actual current requirements of world commerce, and is also capable of deliberate expansion and contraction to offset deflationary and inflationary tendencies in effective world demand.

(d) We need a system possessed of an internal stabilising mechanism, by which pressure is exercised on any country whose balance of payments with the rest of the world is departing from equilibrium *in either direction*, so as to prevent movements which must create for its neighbours an equal but opposite want of balance.

(e) We need an agreed plan for starting off every country after the war with a stock of reserves appropriate to its importance in world commerce, so that without due anxiety it can set its house in order during the transitional period to full peace-time conditions.

(f) We need a central institution, of a purely technical and non-political character, to aid and support other international institutions concerned with the planning and regulation of the world's economic life.

(g) More generally, we need a means of reassurance to a troubled world, by which any country whose own affairs are conducted with due prudence is relieved of anxiety for causes which are not of its own making, concerning its ability to meet its international liabilities; and which will, therefore, make unnecessary those methods of restriction and discrimination which countries have adopted hitherto, not on their merits, but as measures of self-protection from disruptive outside forces.

2. There is also a growing measure of agreement about the general character of any solution of the problem likely to be successful. The particular proposals set forth below lay no claim to originality. They are an attempt to reduce to practical shape certain general ideas belonging to the contemporary climate of economic opinion, which have been given publicity in recent months by writers of several different nationalities. It is difficult to see how any plan can be successful which does not use these general ideas, which are born of the spirit of the age. The actual details put forward below are offered, with no dogmatic intention, as the basis of discussion for criticism and improvement. For we cannot make progress without embodying the general underlying idea in a frame of actual working, which will bring out the practical and political difficulties to be faced and met if the breath of life is to inform it.

3. In one respect this particular plan will be found to be more ambitious and yet, at the same time, perhaps more workable than some of the variant versions of the same basic idea, in that it is fully international, in being based on one general agreement and not on a multiplicity of bilateral arrangements. Doubtless proposals might be made by which bilateral arrangements could be fitted together so as to obtain some of the advantages of a multilateral scheme. But there will be many difficulties attendant on such adjustments. It may be doubted whether a comprehensive scheme will ever in fact be worked out, unless it can come into existence through a single act of creation made possible by the unity of purpose and energy of hope for better things to come, springing from the victory of the United Nations, when they have attained it, over immediate evil. That these proposals are ambitious is claimed, therefore to be not a drawback but an advantage.

4. The proposal is to establish a Currency Union, here designated an *International Clearing Union*, based on international bank money, called (let us say) *bancor*, fixed (but not unalterably) in terms of gold and accepted as the equivalent of gold by the British Commonwealth and the United States and all the other members of the Union for the purpose of settling international balances. The central Banks of all member States (and also of non-members) would keep accounts with the International Clearing Union through which they would be entitled to settle their exchange balances with one another at their par value as defined in terms of bancor. Countries having a favourable balance of payments with the rest of the world as a whole would find themselves in possession of a credit account with the Clearing Union, and those having an unfavourable balance would have a debit account. Measures would be necessary (see below) to prevent the piling up of credit and debit balances without limit, and the system would have failed in the long run if it did not possess sufficient capacity for self-equilibrium to secure this.

5. The idea underlying such a Union is simple, namely, to generalise the essential principle of banking as it is exhibited within any closed system. This principle is the necessary equality of credits and debits. If no credits can be removed outside the clearing system, but only transferred within it, the Union can never be in any difficulty as regards the honouring of cheques drawn upon it. It can make what advances it wishes to any of its members with the assurance that the proceeds can only be transferred to the clearing account of another member. Its sole task is to see to it that its members keep the rules and that the advances made to each of them are prudent and advisable for the Union as a whole.

II – THE PROVISIONS OF THE PLAN

6. The provisions proposed (the particular proportions and other details suggested being tentative as a basis of discussion)

are the following:

(1) All the United Nations will be invited to become original members of the International Clearing Union. Other States may be invited to join subsequently. If ex-enemy States are invited to join, special conditions may be applied to them.

(2) The Governing Board of the Clearing Union shall be appointed by the Governments of the several member States (as provided in (12) below); the daily business with the Union and the technical arrangements being carried out through their Central Banks or other appropriate authorities.

(3) The member States will agree between themselves the initial values of their own currencies in terms of bancor. A member State may not subsequently alter the value of its currency in terms of bancor without the permission of the Governing Board except under the conditions stated below; but during that first five years after the inception of the system the Governing Board shall give special consideration to appeals for an adjustment in the exchange value of a national currency unit on the ground of unforeseen circumstances.

(4) The value of bancor in terms of gold shall be fixed by the Governing Board. Member States shall not purchase or acquire gold, directly or indirectly, at a price in terms of their national currencies in excess of the parity which corresponds to the value of their currency in terms of bancor and to the value of bancor in terms of gold. Their sales and purchases of gold shall not be otherwise restricted.

(5) Each member State shall have assigned to it a *quota*, which shall determine the measure of its responsibility in the management of the Union and of its right to enjoy the credit facilities provided by the Union. The initial quotas might be fixed by reference to the sum of each country's exports and imports on the average of (say) the pre-war years, and might be (say) 75 per cent. of this amount, a special assessment being substituted in cases (of which there might be several) where this formula would be, for any reason, inappropriate. Subsequently, after the elapse

of the transitional period, the quotas should be revised annually in accordance with the running average of each country's actual volume of trade in the three preceding years, rising to a five-year average when figures for five post-war years are available.The determination of a country's quota primarily by reference to the value of its foreign trade seems to offer the criterion most relevant to a plan which is chiefly concerned with the regulation of the foreign exchanges and of a country's international trade balance. It is, however, a matter for discussion whether the formula for fixing quotas should also take account of other factors.

(6) Member States shall agree to accept payment of currency balances, due to them from other members, by a transfer of bancor to their credit in the books of the Clearing Union. They shall be entitled, subject to the conditions set forth below, to make transfers of bancor to other members which have the effect of overdrawing their own accounts with the Union, provided that the maximum debit balances thus created do not exceed their quota. The Clearing Union may, at its discretion, charge a small commission or transfer fee in respect of transactions in its books for the purpose of meeting its current expenses or any other outgoings approved by the Governing Board.

(7) A member State shall pay to the Reserve Fund of the Clearing Union a charge of 1 per cent. per annum on the amount of its average balance in bancor, whether it is a credit or a debit balance, in excess of a quarter of its quota; and a further charge of 1 per cent. on its average balance, whether credit or debit, in excess of a half of its quota. Thus, only a country which keeps as nearly as possible in a state of international balance on the average of the year will escape this contribution. These charges are not absolutely essential to the scheme. But if they are found acceptable, they would be valuable and important inducements towards keeping a level balance, and a significant indication that the system looks on excessive credit balances with as critical an eye as on excessive debit balances, each being, indeed, the inevitable concommitant of the other. Any member State in debit

may, after consultation with the Governing Board, borrow bancor from the balances of any member State in credit on such terms as may be mutually agreed, by which means each would avoid these contributions. The Government Board may, at its discretion, remit the charges on credit balances, and increase correspondingly those on debit balances, if in its opinion unduly expansionist conditions are impending in the world economy.

(8) – (a) A member State may not increase its debit balance by more than a *quarter* of its quota within a year without the permission of the Governing Board. If its debit balance has exceeded a quarter of its quota on the average of at least two years, it shall be entitled to reduce the value of its currency in terms of bancor provided that the reduction shall not exceed 5 per cent. without the consent of the Governing Board; but it shall not be entitled to repeat this procedure unless the Board is satisfied that this procedure is appropriate.

(b) The Governing Board may require from a member State having a debit balance reaching a *half* of its quota the deposit of suitable collateral against its debit balance. Such collateral shall, at the discretion of the Governing Board, take the form of gold, foreign or domestic currency or Government bonds, within the capacity of the member State. As a condition of allowing a member State to increase its debit balance to a figure in excess of a half of its quota, the Governing Board may require all or any of the following measures:

(i) a stated reduction in the value of the member's currency, if it deems that to be the suitable remedy;
(ii) the control of outward capital transactions if not already in force;
(iii) the outright surrender of a suitable proportion of any separate gold or other liquid reserve in reduction of its debit balance.

Furthermore, the Governing Board may recommend to the Government of the member State any internal measures affecting its domestic economy which may appear to be appropriate to restore the equilibiurm of its international balance.

(c) If a member State's debit balance has exceeded *three-quarters* of its quota on the average of at least a year and is excessive in the opinion of the Governing Board in relation to the total debit balances outstanding on the books of the Clearing Union, or is increasing at an excessive rate, it may, in addition, be asked by the Governing Board to take measures to improve its position, and, in the event of its failing to reduce its debit balance accordingly within two years, the Governing Board may declare that it is in default and no longer entitled to draw against its account except with the permission of the Governing Board.

(d) Each member State, on joining the system, shall agree to pay to the Clearing Union any payments due from it to a country in default towards the discharge of the latter's debit balance and to accept this arrangement in the event of falling into default itself. A member State which resigns from the Clearing Union without making approved arrangements for the discharge of any debit balance shall also be treated as in default.

(9) A member State whose credit balance has exceeded a *half* of its quota on the average of at least a year shall discuss with the Governing Board (but shall retain the ultimate decision in its own hands) what measures would be appropriate to restore the equilibrium of its international balances, including:

(a) Measures for the expansion of domestic credit and domestic demand.
(b) The appreciation of its local currency in terms of bancor, or, alternatively the encouragement of an increase in money rates of earnings;
(c) The reduction of tariffs and other discouragements against imports.
(d) International development loans.

(10) A member State shall be entitled to obtain a credit balance in terms of bancor by paying in gold to the Clearing

Union for the credit of its clearing account. But no one is entitled to demand gold from the Union against a balance of bancor, since such balance is available only for transfer to another clearing account. The Governing Board of the Union shall, however, have the discretion to distribute any gold in the possession of the Union between the members possessing credit balances in excess of a specified proportion of their quotas, proportionately to such balances, in reduction of their amount in excess of that proportion.

(11) The monetary reserves of a member State, viz., the Central Bank or other bank or Treasury deposits in excess of a working balance, shall not be held in another country except with the approval of the monetary authorities of that country.

(12) The Governing Board shall be appointed by the Governments of the member States, those with the larger quotas being entitled to appoint a member individually, and those with smaller quotas appointing in convenient political or geographical groups, so that the members would not exceed (say) 12 or 15 in number. Each representative on the Governing Board shall have a vote in proportion to the quotas of the State (or States) appointing him, except that on a proposal to increase a particular quota, a representative's voting power shall be measured by the quotas of the member States appointing him, increased by their credit balance or decreased by their debit balance, averaged in each case over the past two years. Each member State, which is not individually represented on the Governing Board, shall be entitled to appoint a permanent delegate to the Union to maintain contact with the Board and to act as *liason* for daily business and for the exchange of information with the Executive of the Union. Such delegate shall be entitled to be present at the Governing Board when any matter is under consideration which specially concerns the State he represents, and to take part in the discussion.

(13) The Governing Board shall be entitled to reduce the quotas of members, all in the same specified proportion, if it seems necessary to correct in this manner an excess of world

purchasing power. In that event, the provisions of 6 (8) shall be held to apply to the quotas as so reduced, provided that no member shall be required to reduce his actual overdraft at the date of the change, or be entitled by reason of this reduction to alter the value of his currency under 6 (8) (a), except after the expiry of two years. If the Governing Board subsequently desires to correct a potential deficiency of world purchasing power, it shall be entitled to restore the general level of quotas towards the original level.

(14) The Governing Board shall be entitled to ask and receive from each member State any relevant statistical or other information, including a full disclosure of gold, external credit and debit balances and other external assets and liabilities, both public and private. So far as circumstances permit, it will be desirable that the member States shall consult with the Governing Board on important matters of policy likely to affect substantially their bancor balances or their financial relations with other members.

(15) Executive offices of the Union shall be situated in London and New York, with the Governing Board meeting alternately in London and Washington.

(16) Members shall be entitled to withdraw from the Union on a year's notice, subject to their making satisfactory arrangements to discharge any debit balance. They would not, of course, be able to employ any credit balance except by making transfers from it, either before or after their withdrawal, to the Clearing Accounts of other Central Banks. Similarly, it should be within the power of the Governing Board to require the withdrawal of a member, subject to the same notice, if the latter is in breach of agreements relating to the Clearing Union.

(17) The Central Banks of non-member States would be allowed to keep credit clearing accounts with the Union; and, indeed, it would be advisable for them to do so for the conduct of their trade with member States. But they would have no right to overdrafts and no say in the management.

(18) The Governing Board shall make an annual Report and hall convene an annual Assembly at which every member State hall be entitled to be represented individually and to move pro-osals. The principles and governing rules of the Union shall be he subject of reconsideration after five years' experience, if a najority of the Assembly desire it.

II – WHAT LIABILITIES OUGHT THE PLAN TO PLACE ON CREDITOR COUNTRIES?

7. It is not contemplated that either the debit or the credit palance of an individual country ought to exceed a certain naximum—let us say, its *quota*. In the case of debit balances this naximum has been made a rigid one, and, indeed, counter-neasures are called for long before the maximum is reached. In he case of credit balances no rigid maximum has been proposed. For the appropriate provision might be to require the eventual cancellation or compulsory investment of persistent pancor credit balances accumulating in excess of a member's quota; and, however desirable this may be in principle, it might pe felt to impose on creditor countries a heavier burden than hey can be asked to accept before having had experience of the penefit to them of the working of the plan as a whole. If, on the other hand, the limitation were to take the form of the creditor country not being required to accept bancor in excess of a pres-cribed figure, this might impair the general acceptability of pancor, whilst at the same time conferring no real benefit on the creditor country itself. For, if it chose to avail itself of the limita-ion, it must either restrict its exports or be driven back on some form of bilateral payments agreements outside the Clearing Union, thus substituting a less acceptable asset for bancor palances which are based on the collective credit of all the member States and are available for payments to any of them, or attempt the probably temporary expedient of refusing to trade except on a gold basis.

8. The absence of a rigid maximum to credit balances does not impose on any member State, as might be supposed at first sight, an unlimited liability outside its own control. The liability of an individual member is determined, not by the quotas of the other members, but by its own policy in controlling its favourable balance of payments. The existence of the Clearing Union does not deprive a member State of any of the facilities which it now possesses for receiving payment for its exports. In the absence of the Clearing Union a creditor country can employ the proceeds of its exports to buy goods or to buy investments, or to make temporary advances and to hold temporary overseas balances, or to buy gold in the market. All these facilities will remain at its disposal. The difference is that in the absence of the Clearing Union, more or less automatic factors come into play to restrict the volume of its exports after the above means of receiving payment for them have been exhausted. Certain countries become unable to buy and, in addition to this, there is an automatic tendency towards a general slump in international trade and, as a result, a reduction in the exports of the creditor country. Thus, the effect of the Clearing Union is to give the creditor country a choice between voluntarily curtailing its exports to the same extent that they would have been involuntarily curtailed in the absence of the Clearing Union, or, alternatively, of allowing its exports to continue and accumulating the excess receipts in the form of bancor balances for the time being. Unless the removal of a factor causing the involuntary reduction of exports is reckoned a disadvantage, a creditor country incurs no burden but is, on the contrary, relieved, by being offered the additional option of receiving payment for its exports through the accumulation of a bancor balance.

9. If, therefore, a member State asks what governs the maximum liability which it incurs by entering the system, the answer is that this lies entirely within its own control. No more is asked of it than that it should hold in bancor such surplus of its favourable balance of payments as it does not itself choose to employ in any other way, and only for so long as it does not so choose.

IV – SOME ADVANTAGES OF THE PLAN

10. The plan aims at the substitution of an expanionist, in place of a contractionist, pressure on world trade.

11. It effects this by allowing to each member State overdraft facilities of a defined amount. Thus each country is allowed a certain margin of resources and a certain interval of time within which to effect a balance in its economic relations with the rest of the world. These facilities are made possible by the constitution of the system itself and do not involve particular indebtedness between one member State and another. A country is in credit or debit with the Clearing Union as a whole. This means that the overdraft facilities, whilst a relief to some, are not a real burden to others. For the accumulation of a credit balance with the Clearing Union would resemble the importation of gold in signifying that the country holding it is abstaining voluntarily from the immediate use of purchasing power. But it would not involve, as would the importation of gold, the withdrawal of this purchasing power from circulation or the exercise of a deflationary and contractionist pressure on the whole world, including in the end the creditor country itself. Under the proposed plan, therefore, no country suffers injury (but on the contrary) by the fact that the command over resources, which it does not itself choose to employ for the time being, is not withdrawn from use. The accumulation of bancor credit does not curtail in the least its capacity or inducement either to produce or to consume.

12. In short, the analogy with a national banking system is complete. No depositor in a local bank suffers because the balances, which he leaves idle, are employed to finance the business of someone else. Just as the development of national banking systems served to offset a deflationary pressure which would have prevented otherwise the development of modern industry, so by extending the same principle into the international field we may hope to offset the contractionist pressure which might otherwise overwhelm in social disorder and dis-

appointment the good hopes of our modern world. The substitu
tion of a credit mechanism in place of hoarding would have
repeated in the international field the same miracle, already per
formed in the domestic field, of turning a stone into bread.

13. There might be other ways of effecting the same object
temporarily or in part. For example, the United States migh
redistribute her gold. Or there might be a number of bilatera
arrangements having the effect of providing international over
drafts, as, for example, an agreement by the Federal Reserve
Board to accumulate, if necessary, a large sterling balance at the
Bank of England, accompanied by a great number of simila
bilateral arrangements, amounting to some hundreds altogether
between these and all the other banks in the world. The objection
to particular arrangements of this kind, in addition to thei
greater complexity, is that they are likely to be influenced b
extraneous, political reasons; that they put individual countrie
in a position of particular obligation towards others; and that the
distribution of the assistance between different countries ma
not correspond to need and to the real requirements, which ar
extremely difficult to foresee.

14. It should be much easier, and surely more satisfactory fo
all of us, to enter into a general and collective responsibility
applying to all countries alike, that a country finding itself in a
creditor position *against the rest of the world as a whole* should ente
into an arrangement not to allow this credit balance to exercise a
contractionist pressure against world economy and, by repercus
sion, against the economy of the creditor country itself. Thi
would give everyone the great assistance of multilateral clearing
whereby (for example) Great Britain could offset favourabl
balances arising out of her exports to Europe against unfavour
able balances due to the United States or South America o
elsewhere. How, indeed, can any country hope to start up trade
with Europe during the relief and reconstruction period on an
other terms?

15. The facilities offered will be of particular importance in
the transitional period after the war, as soon as the initial shor

tages of supply have been overcome. Many countries will find a difficulty in paying for their imports, and will need time and resources before they can establish a readjustment. The efforts of each of these debtor countries to preserve its own equilibrium, by forcing its exports and by cutting off all imports which are not strictly necessary, will aggravate the problems of all the others. On the other hand, if each feels free from undue pressure, the volume of international exchange will be increased and everyone will find it easier to re-establish equilibrium without injury to the standard of life anywhere. The creditor countries will benefit, hardly less than the debtors, by being given an interval of *time* in which to adjust their economies, during which they can safely move at their own pace without the result of exercising deflationary pressure on the rest of the world, and, by repercussion, on themselves.

16. It must, however, be emphasised that the provision by which the members of the Clearing Union start with substantial overdraft facilities in hand will be mainly useful, just as the possession of any kind of reserve is useful, to allow time and method for necessary adjustments and a comfortable safeguard behind which the unforeseen and the unexpected can be faced with equanimity. Obviously, it does not by itself provide any long-term solution against a continuing disequilibrium, for in due course the more improvident and the more impecunious, left to themselves, would have run through their resources. But if the purpose of the overdraft facilities is mainly to give time for adjustments, we have to make sure, so far as possible, that they *will* be made. We must have, therefore, some rules and some machinery to secure that equilibrum is restored. A tentative attempt to provide for this has been made above. Perhaps it might be strengthened and improved.

17. The provisions suggested differ in one important respect from the pre-war system because they aim at putting some part of the responsibility for adjustment on the creditor country as well as on the debtor. This is an attempt to recover one of the advantages which were enjoyed in the nineteenth century, when

a flow of gold due to a favourable balance in favour of London and Paris, which were then the main creditor centres, immediately produced an expansionist pressure and increased foreign lending in those markets, but which has been lost since New York succeeded to the position of main creditor, as a result of gold movements failing in their effect, of the breakdown of international borrowing and of the frequent flight of loose funds from one depository to another. The object is that the creditor should not be allowed to remain entirely passive. For if he is, an intolerably heavy task may be laid on the debtor country, which is already for that very reason in the weaker position.

18. If, indeed, a country lacks the productive capacity to maintain its standard of life, then a reduction in this standard is not avoidable. If its wage and price levels in terms of money are out of line with those elsewhere, a change in the rate of its foreign exchange is inevitable. But if, possessing the productive capacity it lacks markets because of restrictive policies throughout the world, then the remedy lies in expanding its opportunities for export by removal of the restrictive pressure. We are too ready today to assume the inevitability of unbalanced trade positions thus making the opposite error to those who assumed the tendency of exports and imports to equality. It used to be supposed, without sufficient reason, that effective demand is always properly adjusted throughout the world; we now tend to assume, equally without sufficient reason, that it never can be. On the contrary, there is great force in the contention that, if active employment and ample purchasing power can be sustained in the main centres of the world trade, the problem of surpluses and unwanted exports will largely disappear, even though, under the most prosperous conditions, there may remain some disturbances of trade and unforeseen situations requiring special remedies.

V – THE DAILY MANAGEMENT OF THE EXCHANGES UNDER THE PLAN

19. The Clearing Union restores unfettered multilateral clearing between its members. Compare this with the difficulties

and complications of a large number of bilateral agreements. Compare, above all, the provisions by which a country, taking improper advantage of a payments agreement (for the system is, in fact, a *generalised* payments agreement), as Germany did before the war, is dealt with not by a single country (which may not be strong enough to act effectively in isolation or cannot afford to incur the diplomatic odium of isolated action), but by the system as a whole. If the argument is used that the Clearing Union may have difficulty in disciplining a misbehaving country and in avoiding consequential loss, with what much greater force can we urge this objection against a multiplicity of separate bilateral payments agreements.

20. Thus we should not only obtain the advantages, without the disadvantages, of an international gold currency, but we might enjoy these advantages more widely than was ever possible in practice with the old system under which at any given time only a minority of countries were actually working with free exchanges. In conditions of multilateral clearing, exchange dealings would be carried on as freely as in the best days of the gold standard, without its being necessary to ask anyone to accept special or onerous conditions.

21. The principles governing transactions are: first, that the Clearing Union is set up, not for the transaction of daily business between individual traders or banks, but for the clearing and settlement of the ultimate outstanding balances between Central Banks (and certain other super-national Institutions), such as would have been settled under the old gold standard by the shipment or the earmarking of gold, and should not trespass unnecessarily beyond this field; and, second, that its purpose is to increase *freedom* in international commerce and not to multiply interferences or compulsions.

22. Many central Banks have found great advantage in centralising with themselves or with an Exchange Control the supply and demand of all foreign exchange, thus dispensing with an outside exchange market, though continuing to accommodate individuals through the existing banks and not directly.

The further extension of such arrangements would be consonant with the general purposes of the Clearing Union, inasmuch as they would promote order and discipline in international exchange transactions in detail as well as in general. The same is true of the control of Capital Movements, further described below, which many States are likely to wish to impose on their own nationals. But the structure of the proposed Clearing Union does not *require* such measures of centralisation or of control on the part of a member State. It is, for example, consistent alike with the type of Exchange Control now established in the United Kingdom or with the system now operating in the United States. The Union does not prevent private holdings of foreign currency or private dealings in exchange or international capital movements, if these have been approved or allowed by the member States concerned. Central Banks can deal direct with one another as heretofore. No transaction in bancor will take place except when a member State or its Central Bank is exercising the right to pay in it. In no case is there any direct control of capital movements by the Union, even in the case of 6 (8) (b) (ii) above, but only by the member States themselves through their own institutions. Thus the fabric of international banking organisation, built up by long experience to satisfy practical needs, would be left as undisturbed as possible.

23. It is not necessary to interfere with the discretion of countries which desire to maintain a special intimacy within a particular group of countries associated by geographical or political ties, such as the existing sterling area, or groups, like the Latin Union of former days, which may come into existence covering, for example, the countries of North America or those of South America, or the groups now under active discussion, including Poland and Czechoslovakia or certain of the Balkan States. There is no reason why such countries should not be allowed a double position, both as members of the Clearing Union in their own right with their proper quota, and also as making use of another financial centre along traditional lines, as, for example, Australia and India with London, or certain American countries with New York. In this case, their accounts with the Clearing Union would

be in exactly the same position as the independent gold reserves which they now maintain, and they would have no occasion to modify in any way their present practices in the conduct of daily business.

24. There might be other cases, however, in which a dependency or a member of a federal union would merge its currency identity in that of a mother country, with a quota appropriately adjusted to the merged currency area as a whole, and *not* enjoy a separate individual membership of the Clearing Union, as, for example, the States of a Federal Union, the French colonies or the British Crown Colonies.

25. At the same time countries, which do not belong to a special geographical or political group, would be expected to keep their reserve balances with the Clearing Union and not with one another. It has, therefore, been laid down that balances may not be held in another country except with the approval of the monetary authorities of that country; and, in order that sterling and dollars might not appear to compete with bancor for the purpose of reserve balances, the United Kingdom and the United States might agree together that they would not accept the reserve balances of other countries in excess of normal working balances except in the case of banks definitely belonging to a Sterling Area or Dollar Area group.

VI – THE POSITION OF GOLD UNDER THE PLAN

26. Gold still possesses great psychological value which is not being diminished by current events; and the desire to possess a gold reserve against unforeseen contingencies is likely to remain. Gold also has the merit of providing in point of form (whatever the underlying realities may be) an uncontroversial standard of value for international purposes, for which it would not yet be easy to find a serviceable substitute. Moreover, by supplying an automatic means for settling some part of the favourable balances of the creditor countries, the current gold production of the world and the remnant of gold reserves held outside the

United States may still have a useful part to play. Nor is it reasonable to ask the United States to de-monetise the stock of gold which is the basis of its impregnable liquidity. What, in the long run, the world may decide to do with gold is another matter. The purpose of the Clearing Union is to supplant gold as a governing factor, but not to dispense with it.

27. The international bank-money which we have designated *bancor* is defined in terms of a weight of gold. Since the national currencies of the member States are given a defined exchange value in terms of bancor, it follows that they would each have a defined gold content which would be their official buying price for gold, above which they must not pay. The fact that a member State is entitled to obtain a credit in terms of bancor by paying actual gold to the credit of its clearing account, secures a steady and ascertained purchaser for the output of the gold-producing countries, and for countries holding a large reserve of gold. Thus the position of producers and holders of gold is not affected adversely, and is, indeed, improved.

28. Central Banks would be entitled to retain their separate gold reserves and ship gold to one another, provided they did not pay a price above parity; they could coin gold and put it into circulation, and, generally speaking, do what they liked with it.

29. One limitation only would be, for obvious reasons, essential. No member State would be entitled to demand gold from the Clearing Union against its balance of bancor; for bancor is available only for transfer to another clearing account. Thus between gold and bancor itself there would be a one-way convertibility, such as ruled frequently before the war with national currencies which were on what was called a 'gold exchange standard'. This need not mean that the Clearing Union would only receive gold and never pay it out. It has been provided above that, if the Clearing Union finds itself in possession of a stock of gold, the Governing Board shall have discretion to distribute the surplus between those possessing credit balances in bancor, proportionately to such balances in reduction of their amount.

30. The question has been raised whether these arrangements are compatible with the retention by individual member states of a full gold standard with two-way convertibility, so that, for example, any foreign central bank acquiring dollars could use them to obtain gold for export. It is not evident that a good purpose would be served by this. But it need not be prohibited, and if any member State should prefer to maintain full convertibility for interval purposes it could protect itself from any abuse of the system or inconvenient consequences by providing that gold could only be exported under licence.

31. The value of bancor in terms of gold is fixed but not unalterably. The power to vary its value might have to be exercised if the stocks of gold tendered to the Union were to be excessive. No object would be served by attempting to peer into the future or to prophesy the ultimate outcome.

VII – THE CONTROL OF CAPITAL MOVEMENTS

32. There is no country which can, in future, safely allow the flight of funds for political reasons or to evade domestic taxation or in anticipation of the owner turning refugee. Equally, there is no country that can safely receive fugitive funds, which constitute an unwanted import of capital, yet cannot safely be used for fixed investment.

33. For these reasons it is widely held that control of capital movements, both inward and outward, should be a permanent feature of the post-war system. It is an objection to this that control, if it is to be effective, probably requires the machinery of exchange control for *all* transactions, even though a general permission is given to all remittances in respect of current trade. Thus those countries which have for the time being no reason to fear, and may indeed welcome, outward capital movements, may be reluctant to impose this machinery, even though a general permission for capital, as well as current, transactions reduces it to being no more than a machinery of record. On the

other hand, such control will be more difficult to work by unilateral action on the part of those countries which cannot afford to dispense with it, especially in the absence of a postal censorship, if movements of capital cannot be controlled *at both ends*. It would, therefore, be of great advantage if the United States, as well as other members of the Clearing Union, would adopt machinery similar to that which the British Exchange Control has now gone a long way towards perfecting. Nevertheless, the universal establishment of a control of capital movements cannot be regarded as essential to the operation of the Clearing Union; and the method and degree of such control should therefore be left to the decision of each member State. Some less drastic way might be found by which countries, not themselves controlling outward capital movements, can deter inward movements not approved by the countries from which they originate.

34. The position of abnormal balances in overseas ownership held in various countries at the end of the war presents a problem of considerable importance and special difficulty. A country in which a large volume of such balances is held could not, unless it is in a creditor position, afford the risk of having to redeem them in bancor on a substantial scale, if this would have the effect of depleting its bancor resources at the outset. At the same time, it is very desirable that the countries owning these balances should be able to regard them as liquid, at any rate over and above the amounts which they can afford to lock up under an agreed programme of funding or long-term expenditure. Perhaps there should be some special over-riding provision for dealing with the transitional period only by which, through the aid of the Clearing Union, such balances would remain liquid and convertible into bancor by the creditor country whilst there would be no corresponding strain on the bancor resources of the debtor country, or, at any rate, the resulting strain would be spread over a period.

35. The advocacy of a control of capital movements must not be taken to mean that the era of international investment should

be brought to an end. On the contrary, the system contemplated should greatly facilitate the restoration of international loans and credits for legitimate purposes. The object, and it is a vital object, is to have a means:

(a) of distinguishing long-term loans by creditor countries, which help to maintain equilibrium and develop the world's resources, from movements of funds out of debtor countries which lack the means to finance them; and
(b) of controlling short-term speculative movements or flights of currency whether out of debtor countries or from one creditor country to another.

36. It should be emphasised that the purpose of the overdrafts of bancor permitted by the Clearing Union is, not to facilitate long-term, or even medium-term, credits to be made by debtor countries which cannot afford them, but to allow time and a breathing space for adjustments and for averaging one period with another to all member States alike, whether in the long run they are well-placed to develop a forward international loan policy or whether their prospects of profitable new development in excess of their own resources justifies them in long-term borrowing. The machinery and organisation of international medium-term and long-term lending is another aspect of postwar economic policy, not less important than the purposes which the Clearing Union seeks to serve, but requiring another, complementary institution.

VIII – RELATION OF THE CLEARING UNION TO COMMERCIAL POLICY

37. The special protective expedients which were developed between the two wars were sometimes due to political, social or industrial reasons. But frequently they were nothing more than forced and undesired dodges to protect an unbalanced position of a country's overseas payments. The new system, by helping to provide a register of the size and whereabouts of the aggregate

debtor and creditor positions respectively, and an indication whether it is reasonable for a particular country to adopt special expedients as a temporary measure to assist in regaining equilibrium in its balance of payments, would make it possible to establish a general rule *not* to adopt them, subject to the indicated exceptions.

38. The existence of the Clearing Union would make it possible for member States contracting commercial agreements to use their respective debit and credit positions with the Clearing Union as a test, though this test by itself would not be complete. Thus, the contracting parties, whilst agreeing to clauses in a commercial agreement forbidding, in general, the use of certain measures or expedients in their mutual trade relations, might make this agreement subject to special relaxations if the state of their respective clearing accounts satisfied an agreed criterion. For example, an agreement might provide that, in the event of one of the contracting States having a debit balance with the Clearing Union exceeding a specified proportion of its quota on the average of a period it should be free to resort to import regulation or to barter trade agreements or to higher import duties of a type which was restricted under the agreement in normal circumstances. Protected by the possibility of such temporary indulgences, the members of the Clearing Union should feel much more confidence in moving towards the withdrawal of other and more dislocating forms of protection and discrimination and in accepting the prohibition of the worst of them from the outset. In any case, it should be laid down that members of the Union would not allow or suffer among themselves any restrictions on the disposal of receipts arising out of current trade or 'invisible' income.

IX – THE USE OF THE CLEARING UNION FOR OTHER INTERNATIONAL PURPOSES

39. The Clearing Union might become the instrument and the support of international policies in addition to those which it

is its primary purpose to promote. This deserves the greatest possible emphasis. The Union might become the pivot of the future economic government of the world. Without it, other more desirable developments will find themselves impeded and unsupported. With it, they will fall into their place as parts of an ordered scheme. No one of the following suggestions is a necessary part of the plan. But they are illustrations of the additional purposes of high importance and value which the Union, once established, might be able to serve:

(1) The Union might set up a clearing account in favour of international bodies charged with post-war relief, rehabilitation and reconstruction. But it could go much further than this. For it might supplement contributions received from other sources by granting preliminary overdraft facilities in favour of these bodies, the overdraft being discharged over a period of years out of the Reserve Fund of the Union, or, if necessary, out of a levy on surplus credit balances. So far as this method is adopted it would be possible to avoid asking any country to assume a burdensome commitment for relief and reconstruction, since the resources would be provided in the first instance by those countries having credit clearing accounts for which they have no immediate use and are voluntarily leaving idle, and in the long run by those countries which have a chronic international surplus for which they have no beneficial employment.

(2) The Union might set up an account in favour of any supernational policing body which may be charged with the duty of preserving the peace and maintaining international order. If any country were to infringe its properly authorised orders, the policing body might be entitled to request the Governors of the Clearing Union to hold the clearing account of the delinquent country to its order and permit no further transactions on the account except by its authority. This would provide an excellent machinery for enforcing a financial blockade.

(3) The Union might set up an account in favour of international bodies charged with the management of a Commodity Control, and might finance stocks of commodities held by such

bodies, allowing them overdraft facilities on their accounts up to an agreed maximum. By this means the financial problem of buffer stocks and 'ever-normal granaries' could be effectively attacked.

(4) The Union might be linked up with a Board for International Investment. It might act on behalf of such a Board and collect for them the annual service of their loans by automatically debiting the clearing accounts of the country concerned. The statistics of the clearing accounts of the member States would give a reliable indication as to which countries were in a position to finance the Investment Board, with the advantage of shifting the whole system of clearing credits and debits nearer to equilibrium.

(5) There are various methods by which the Clearing Union could use its influence and its powers to maintain stability of prices and to control the Trade Cycle. If an International Economic Board is established, this Board and the Clearing Union might be expected to work in close collaboration to their mutual advantage. If an International Investment or Development Corporation is also set up together with a scheme of Commodity Controls for the control of stocks of the staple primary products, we might come to possess in these three Institutions a powerful means of combating the evils of the Trade Cycle, by exercising contractionist or expansionist influence on the system as a whole or on particular sections. This is a large and important question which cannot be discussed adequately in this paper; and need not be examined at length in this place because it does not raise any important issues affecting the fundamental constitution of the proposed Union. It is mentioned here to complete the picture of the wider purposes which the foundation of the Clearing Union might be made to serve.

40. The facility of applying the Clearing Union plan to these several purposes arises out of a fundamental characteristic which is worth pointing out, since it distinguishes the plan from those proposals which try to develop the same basic principle along

bilateral lines and is one of the grounds on which the Plan can claim superior merit. This might be described as its 'anonymous' or 'impersonal' quality. No particular member States have to engage their own resources as such to the support of other particular States or of any of the international projects or policies adopted. They have only to agree in general that, if they find themselves with surplus resources which for the time being they do not themselves wish to employ, these resources may go into the general pool and be put to work on approved purposes. This costs the surplus country nothing because it is not asked to part permanently, or even for any specified period, with such resources, which it remains free to expend and employ for its own purposes whenever it chooses; in which case the burden of finance is passed on to the next recipient, again for only so long as the recipient has no use for the money. As pointed out above, this merely amounts to extending to the international sphere the methods of any domestic banking system, which are in the same sense 'impersonal' inasmuch as there is no call on the particular depositor either to support as such the purposes for which his banker makes advances or to forgo permanently the use of his deposit. There is no countervailing objection except that which applies equally to the technique of domestic banking, namely that it is capable of the abuse of creating excessive purchasing power and hence an inflation of prices. In our efforts to avoid the opposite evil, we must not lose sight of this risk, to which there is an allusion in 39 (5) above. But it is no more reason for refusing the advantages of international banking than the similar risk in the domestic field is a reason to return to the practices of the seventeenth century goldsmiths (which are what we are still following in the international field) and to forgo the vast expansion of production which banking principles have made possible. Where financial contributions are required for some purpose of general advantage, it is a great facility not to have to ask for specific contributions from any named country, but to depend rather on the anonymous and impersonal aid of the system as a whole. We have here a genuine organ of truly international government.

X – THE TRANSITIONAL ARRANGEMENTS

41. It would be of great advantage to agree the general principles of the Clearing Union before the end of the war, with a view to bringing it into operation at an early date after the termination of hostilities. Major plans will be more easily brought to birth in the first energy of victory and whilst the active spirit of united action still persists, than in the days of exhaustion and reaction from so much effort which may well follow a little later. Such a proposal presents, however, something of a dilemma. On the one hand, many countries will be in particular need of reserves of overseas resources in the period immediately after the war. On the other hand, goods will be in short supply and the prevention of inflationary international conditions of much more importance for the time being than the opposite. The expansionist tendency of the plan, which is a leading recommendation of it as soon as peace-time output is restored and the productive capacity of the world is in running order, might be a danger in the early days of a sellers' market and an excess of demand over supply.

42. A reconciliation of these divergent purposes is not easily found until we know more than is known at present about the means to be adopted to finance post-war relief and reconstruction. If the intention is to provide resources on liberal and comprehensive lines outside the resources made available by the Clearing Union and additional to them, it might be better for such specific aid to take the place of the proposed overdrafts during the 'relief' period of (say) two years. In this case credit clearing balances would be limited to the amount of gold delivered to the Union, and the overdraft facilities created by the Union in favour of the Relief Council, the International Investment Board or the Commodity Controls. Nevertheless, the immediate establishment of the Clearing Union would not be incompatible with provisional arrangements, which could take alternative forms according to the character of the other 'relief' arrangements, qualifying and limiting the overdraft quotas. Overdraft quotas might be allowed on a reduced scale during the

transitional period. Or it might be proper to provide that countries in receipt of relief or Lend-lease assistance should not have access at the same time to overdraft facilities, and that the latter should only become available when the former had come to an end. If, on the other hand, relief from outside sources looks like being inadequate from the outset, the overdraft quotas may be even more necessary at the outset than later on.

43. We must not be over-cautious. A rapid economic restoration may lighten the tasks of the diplomatists and the politicians in the resettlement of the world and the restoration of social order. For Great Britain and other countries outside the 'relief' areas the possibility of exports sufficient to sustain their standard of life is bound up with good and expanding markets. We cannot afford to wait too long for this, and we must not allow excessive caution to condemn us to perdition. Unless the Union is a going concern, the problem of proper 'timing' will be nearly insoluble. It is sufficient at this stage to point out that the problem of timing must not be overlooked, but that the Union is capable of being used so as to aid rather than impede its solution.

XI – CONCLUSION

44. It has been suggested that so ambitious a proposal is open to criticism on the ground that it requires from the members of the Union a greater surrender of their sovereign rights than they will readily concede. But no greater surrender is required than in a commercial treaty. The obligations will be entered into voluntarily and can be terminated on certain conditions by giving notice.

45. A greater readiness to accept super-national arrangements must be required in the post-war world. If the arrangements proposed can be described as a measure of financial disarmament, there is nothing here which we need be reluctant to accept ourselves or to ask of others. It is an advantage, and not a disadvantage, of the scheme that it invites the member States to abandon that

licence to promote indiscipline, disorder and bad-neighbour-liness which, to the general disadvantage, they have been free to exercise hitherto.

46. The plan makes a beginning at the future economic ordering of the world between nations and the 'winning of the peace'. It might help to create the conditions and the atmosphere in which much else would be made easier.

Name and Author Index

179

Subject Index

Nigeria, 39, 44, 132
  capital expenditure programme, 57,
    58, 60-1
  oil exports, 50-1
non-oil exporters, 96-7, 98, 120-3
North-South divide, 3-4, 9-10, 118-44
Nurskean balanced growth, model, 72, 84
Nyasaland, 145

OECD (Organisation for Economic
  Cooperation and Development)
  countries, 79, 118, 119, 123, 129,
    143-4
oil, 50-1, 58, 60, 120, 129
  see also oil-exporters
oil-exporters, 96-7, 131
OPEC (Organisation of Petroleum-
  Exporting Countries), 50, 119, 129
  see also oil-exporters
open general licences, 55, 57, 95
Organisation for Economic Cooperation
  and Development, see OECD
Organisation of Petroleum-Exporting
  countries, see OPEC
output, potential, 40-3, 62-3
overdrafts in ICU, 93, 96-102, 142-3
overloaded investment programmes,
  57-61

par values, 92-4
penalties in ICU, 93, 97
per capita income, 1, 4, 8-10, 40
permits, exchange, see licences
phasing of expenditure, 46, 57
Plain Speaking: An Oral Biography of Harry
  S. Truman (Miller), 141
planned industrialisation, 8
planning development, 44-6, 51-7
'Policy of Government Storage of
  Foodstuffs and Raw Materials, The'
  (Keynes), 22
politics, and cooperation, 134-5
population growth, 10-11, 18-21, 40-2
Post-War External Problems, Committee
  on, 25
potential, economic, 40-3, 62-3, 72
poverty, 3, 9
poverty trap, 40
Prebisch-Singer hypothesis, 11, 73
price mechanism, 56, 132
prices, 11, 22-7, 77-8, 110-11
private exchange markets, 104-5
private sector, 46, 82-4, 125-6, 143-4
productivity, 6, 118-20

progress
  economic, conditions for, 17
  material, 4, 17-18
projects, planning, 43-6, 57-60
protectionism, 74, 123, 140

quotas in ICU, 93, 96-102, 142-3

Reagan Administration, 124, 125, 126
'Recent Economic Events in India'
  (Keynes), 28
recession, 110-11, 128
Reconstruction of Europe (ed. Keynes), 19
reflation, 129
Reserve Fund (ICU), 13
reserves, 98, 107, 111-15
resources, 6, 71-4, 115
restriction of internal demand, 51
Rhodesia, 145
rich-poor country divide, see North-
  South divide
'Rise and Decline of Development
  Economics, The' (Hirschman), 71
risks, 15-16
Romania, 77
Rome, 16-17
Royal Economic Society, 7, 28, 67
rupee, 31
Russian Empire, 134

Saudi Arabia, 85
saving, 42, 47-8
savings gap, 47-8
'scarce currency clause', 155
SDR (Special Drawing Rights) scheme,
  24, 113, 127
Second World War, 6, 22, 68, 119, 141
selectivity of investment, 79-80
Seoul, IMF conference at, 124-6, 127
services, 42-3, 52, 56
shortages, specific, 43, 47, 63
'small country' models, 50
'Some Economic Consequences of a
  Declining Population' (Keynes), 14
Spain, 18
Special Drawing Rights scheme, see SDR
'spending out of depression', 36
Sri Lanka, 77
Stabex, 26
stagflation, 21
State Bank, in India, 30
state intervention, see intervention
stocks, storage of, 22-5, 113
subsidies for storage, 22-3